I0820820

This book should be returned to any branch of the
L~~~~                                    before the da

# AGENT CICERO

Other books by Mark Simmons:

*A Crack in Time: A Search for the Echoes of the American
   Civil War* (2004)

*From the Foam of the Sea* (2007)

*The Serpent and the Cross* (2010)

*The Battle of Matapan 1941: The Trafalgar of the
   Mediterranean* (2011)

*The Rebecca Code: Rommel's Spy in North Africa and
   Operation Kondor* (2012)

*Room 39 and the Cornish Legacy* (2013)

# AGENT CICERO

# HITLER'S MOST SUCCESSFUL SPY

MARK SIMMONS

Dedicated to the memory of that consummate actor, James Mason.

'What is morally wrong can never be advantageous, even when it enables you to make some gain that you believe to be to your advantage. The mere act of believing that some wrongful course of action constitutes an advantage is pernicious.'

'The enemy is within the gates; it is with our own luxury, our own folly, our own criminality that we have to contend.'

'Memory is the treasury and guardian of all things.'

Marcus Tullius Cicero, 106 BC–43 BC

First published 2014
by Spellmount, an imprint of
The History Press
The Mill, Brimscombe Port
Stroud, Gloucestershire, GL5 2QG
www.thehistorypress.co.uk

© Mark Simmons 2014

The right of Mark Simmons to be identified as the Author
of this work has been asserted in accordance with the
Copyright, Designs and Patents Act 1988.

British Library Cataloguing in Publication Data.
A catalogue record for this book is available from the British Library.

ISBN 978 0 7509 5286 6

Typesetting and origination by The History Press
Printed in Great Britain

# CONTENTS

# ACKNOWLEDGEMENTS

The story of Germany's most successful spy came to my attention again, after many years, while engaged in research for my previous non-fiction book, *The Rebecca Code: Rommel's Spy in North Africa and Operation Condor* (Spellmount, 2012). In the book, two German spies, Johannes Eppler and Heinrich Sandstette, are taken by the famed explorer Count László Almásy across the Western Desert and into Cairo to spy on the British Eighth Army HQ. To fund their mission, the *Abwehr* agents are supplied with thousands of pounds sterling, although, unbeknown to them, it is all counterfeit. The Albanian Elyesa Bazna, who later became Agent Cicero, was paid with the same forged money, to the tune of some £300,000, all coming from the Nazi counterfeiting scheme named Operation Bernhard. The Cicero case was something I felt needed looking at again for several reasons.

It had first come to my attention with the feature film *Five Fingers*, starring James Mason as Cicero. I felt the character, portrayed so well by Mason, was a faithful depiction after we were told this was a 'true story'. However, when I came to read L.C. Moyzisch's book, *Operation Cicero* (1950), on which the film was loosely based, it was apparent that *Five Fingers*, as entertaining as it was, was a highly distorted version of the real story. Rereading my battered 1952 Readers Union edition of *Operation Cicero*, it became obvious the story needed updating, as many secret British and American files on the subject are now open to the public.

Moyzisch's book was the first to tell the story; he had been the main link between the Germans and agent Cicero. He is at times guilty of overstating his position and denying mistakes, but then this is a very human frailty. In a postscript to later editions, Franz Von Papen, German ambassador in Turkey and once chancellor of Germany, supports his account.

*Five Fingers* was brought out in 1952 and Von Papen released his memoirs that same year; it has a whole chapter on the Cicero case and much else that bears on it. Elyesa Bazna was the last to release his account in 1961, in a veiled attempt to embarrass the German government into compensating him for the Nazi regime's fraud of having paid him with counterfeit money. He does exaggerate his abilities at times, often wildly, and is guilty of other flights of fantasy.

The British MI5 and MI6 files were released to the public in 2006, while the American CIA released their secret 'Footnote to Cicero' rather earlier in 1994. It was my aim, as it had been with *The Rebecca Code*, to bring together these three eyewitness accounts by Moyzisch, Von Papen and Bazna, along with the official files, and tell the true story of Operation Cicero.

Secondary sources that have been most useful include Sir Hughe Knatchbull-Hugessen's memoirs, *Diplomat in Peace and War* (1949), although, due to the British Official Secrets Act, Knatchbull-Hugessen does not mention Cicero. However, it does provide a portrait of the times and much pertinent information on the delicate situations he was handling.

Walter Schellenberg's *The Memoirs of Hitler's Spymaster* (2006), first published as *The Schellenberg Memoirs: A Record of the Nazi Secret Service* (1956), covered his involvement in the Cicero case, and provided a broader view of the world of Nazi intelligence services and the German High Command.

Anthony Cave Brown's impressive *Body Guard of Lies* (1975) gave me a flavour of much good background material, although without the benefit of secret files his conclusions are questionable.

David Kahn's *The Code Breakers* (1968) and *Hitler's Spies* (1978) supplied many more details.

Richard Wires' *The Cicero Spy Affair* (1999) is one of the few books entirely devoted to the Cicero case, and is an excellent academic treatment.

Adrian Weale's *The SS: A New History* (2010) is a good guide on details of the SS, which he has made his speciality.

I was particularly pleased to obtain a copy of Adolf Burger's book, *The Devil's Workshop: A Memoir of the Nazi Counterfeiting Operation* (2009), and even more so to find it was signed by the author: a clear link to the past and the Cicero case.

I am grateful to staff at Bletchley Park, and even more so to see a room now devoted to the Battle of Matapan after I had written a book on the subject, *The Battle of Matapan* (2011). I thank the staff of the Public Records Office; Dorothy J. Heatts at the Central Intelligence Agency Library; the United States National Archives and Records Administration; the United States Navy Historical Department; the Imperial War Museums; and the Opel Centre, Berlin.

I am hugely indebted to the following people who have given freely of their time: Shaun Barrington, my commissioning editor at The History Press, for his enthusiastic support for the project; Group Captain L.E. (Robbie) Robins CBE AE** DL, another grand supporter, for reading an early draft and making many excellent comments and suggestions; John Sherress, fellow author and good crutch when the going got tough; and my magazine editors, Iain Ballantyne, John Mussell and Flint Whitlock, for continued support.

Finally, as always my wife, Margaret, gave her wholehearted support in the nuts and bolts of building a book, with proofreading, index-compiling, work on the maps, and finding her way through the labyrinth of strange and unfamiliar names, and my creative misspelling of them. Thanks to all.

# DRAMATIS PERSONAE IN BRIEF

Bazna, Elyesa – Albanian/Turkish valet at the British Embassy in Ankara, sometimes known as Diello/Ilya. Spied for the Germans under the codename 'Cicero'.

Dulles, Allen Welsh – American OSS agent in Switzerland. Later director of the CIA.

Garcia, Juan Pujol – Spanish double agent under the British codename 'Garbo' and *Abwehr* codename 'Arabel'.

Kaltenbrunner, Ernst – German SS General. Chief of the RSHA.

Kapp, Cornelia – German translator/secretary, also known as Nele or Elisabet. Spied for the OSS at the German Embassy in Ankara.

Knatchbull-Hugessen, Sir Hughe – British ambassador in Ankara.

Menzies, Sir Stewart Graham – British head of SIS/MI6, also known as 'C'.

Moyzisch, Ludwig Carl – German commercial attaché/SD officer at German Embassy in Ankara.

Von Papen, Franz Joseph – German ambassador in Ankara.

Ribbentrop, Joachim – German Foreign Minister.

Schellenberg, Walter Friedrich – German intelligence officer with the SD, later head of the RSHA.

# GLOSSARY AND ACRONYMS

| | |
|---|---|
| *Abwehr* | German secret service, meaning 'defence' in German. |
| AO | *Abwehr* officer. |
| Bupo | *Bundespolizei*, the Swiss secret police. |
| 'C' | Head of British Secret Intelligence Service (SIS) MI6. |
| Camp 020 | British interrogation centre in Richmond, Surrey. |
| CIA | Central Intelligence Agency, replaced OSS, USA. |
| CID | Committee of Imperial Defence, British. |
| cobbler | *Abwehr* slang for a forger. |
| DCI | Director of Central Intelligence, USA. |
| *Emniyet* | Turkish secret service. |
| Enigma | German code machine system. |
| FBI | Federal Bureau of Investigation, USA. |
| FHW | *Fremde Heere West*, intelligence branch German High Command. |
| FO | Foreign Office, British. |
| *Funkabwehr* | German radio security service. |
| GC & CS | Government Code and Cypher School, Bletchley Park. |
| GCHQ | Government Communications Headquarters. |
| Gestapo | *Geheime Staatspolizei*, German secret state police. |
| GRU | Soviet military intelligence. |
| KGB | Soviet intelligence service. |
| LRDG | Long Range Desert Group, British. |
| MI5 | Military Intelligence section 5. British counter-intelligence service. |
| MI6 | Military Intelligence section 6. British espionage service, often known as SIS. |
| NID | Naval Intelligence Department, British. |
| NKVD | *Narodnyy Kommissariat Vnutrennikh Del*, Soviet secret police. |
| NSA | National Security Agency, USA. |

| | |
|---|---|
| OKH | *Oberkommando des Heeres*, German High Command. |
| OKW | *Oberkommando der Wehrmacht*, German Armed Forces High Command. |
| OSS | Office of Strategic Services, replaced by CIA, USA. |
| RFO | Reich Foreign Office. |
| RSHA | *Reichssicherheitshauptamt*, supreme state security department. Set up in 1939 to supervise the Gestapo and SD. |
| SA | *Sturmabteilung*, or 'Brownshirts'. Paramilitary wing of the Nazi party, replaced by the SS. |
| SBS | Special Boat Service, British. |
| Section D | SIS sabotage section. |
| SD | *Sicherheitsdienst*, secret service branch of the SS. |
| SIM | *Servizio Italiano Militare*, Italian Military Intelligence Service. |
| SIPO | *Sicherheitspolizei*, security police of the Gestapo and SD. |
| SIS | Secret Intelligence Service, British, also known as MI6. |
| Smersh | 'Death to spies', counter-intelligence service of the Red Army. |
| SOE | Special Operations Executive, British Section D of SIS. |
| SS | *Schutzstaffel*, or 'protection squad'. The original title for Hitler's bodyguard. |
| Station X | GC & CS, Bletchley Park. |
| Ultra | Ultra decodes encrypted Axis radio communications classified 'Ultra Secret'. |
| Waffen-SS | Military arm of the SS. |
| Walk-in | Agent as a stranger, freelance, offers services to a particular government often not his own. |

# OFFICER RANKS

| Waffen SS | German Army | British/USA Army |
|---|---|---|
| *SS-Untersturmführer* | *Leutnant* | Second Lieutenant |
| *SS-Obersturmführer* | *Oberleutnant* | Lieutenant |
| *SS-Hauptsturmführer* | *Hauptmann* | Captain |
| *SS-Sturmbannführer* | *Major* | Major |
| *SS-Obersturmbannführer* | *Oberstleutnant* | Lieutenant Colonel |
| *SS-Standartenführer* | *Oberst* | Colonel |
| No equivalent | No equivalent | Brigadier |
| *SS-Brigadeführer* | *Generalmajor* | Major General |
| *SS-Gruppenführer* | *Generalleutnant* | Lieutenant General |
| *SS-Obergruppenführer* | *General* | General |
| *SS-Oberstgruppenführer* | *Generaloberst* | No equivalent |
| No equivalent | *Generalfeldmarschall* | Field Marshal/General of the Army |

# PROLOGUE

## Bovingdon Airfield, England, 11 May 1945

The Douglas C-47 Skytrain of the US Army Air Force (USAAF) made its approach to Bovingdon's main runway from the north-east. The weather was fine on that spring morning, with mist and fog clearing; later it turned cloudy and light rain began to fall. With a screech of tyres on concrete, the great workhorse of the Allied air forces, known affectionately by the Royal Air Force (RAF) as the Dakota, was down.

On board were mainly US personnel beginning their long trip home, starting from Weimar in Germany. Field Marshal Wilhelm Keitel had signed Germany's final act of capitulation only a few days before, and the war in Europe was over. With the GIs and USAAF flyers were a few German nationals who were of sufficient interest to Allied intelligence to warrant being flown to Britain and interviewed in London. One of these was 23-year-old Maria Clara Mathilde Molkenteller, a bright, intelligent young woman who had come to the attention of the Americans.

During her protracted interrogation, Maria insisted she had volunteered; however, the US Army report says she was 'picked up by Halle CIC as a result of information given by an informant'.[1] Both accounts may well be true in the flux that then existed in Germany. Once she was aware the Allied authorities knew of her existence, she may well have come forward of her own volition. The town of Halle is situated in the southern part of Saxony-Anhult on the Saale River, and was in the path of the advancing Red Army; in Allied hands she would be safe and fed, away from the horrors that might await any young German woman.

On 31 March 1945, and again a few days later, Halle was bombed by the Allied air forces, resulting in the deaths of over 1,000 people and the destruction of large areas of the town. As a consequence, it resembled many of the devastated towns and cities of the Third Reich when, on 17 April, Halle was occupied by American troops. The Americans sent Maria to British intelligence, knowing that her story, and the revelation of an agent called Cicero, would be of great interest.

The country Maria arrived in was a total contrast to the country she had left: Britain was consumed by wild celebrations of Victory in Europe, while Germany lay in smouldering ruins. The train journey from Hertfordshire to London would have passed through villages and towns in the throes of jubilation and not devastated by warring armies. The day after her arrival at the female interrogation centre on Nightingale Lane, the city went mad: it was festooned with national flags, fireworks and floodlights illuminating the night sky; Whitehall and the Mall were packed with thousands of people; and even though nothing had been officially announced, the rumour spread that the Jerries had thrown in the towel. As Big Ben struck 3 p.m., Prime Minister Winston Churchill spoke over loudspeakers relayed by outside radio broadcasts to the nation and the British Empire, telling the people that the war in Europe would end at midnight. Maria may or may not have witnessed these scenes, but in London she must have seen areas of damage inflicted by the *Luftwaffe* and the V1 and V2 rockets; however, it was far from the scale her homeland had suffered. Hitler's speeches about the damage inflicted on London were greatly exaggerated.

It was a few days later that her interrogation, led by Captain F. Basett, started. He found out that Maria was born in Naumburg, on the Saale River in Saxony, in 1922. Her father, Otto, was a clergyman who was partially blind all his life. Her mother, Elfrieda, was a native of Halle and the daughter of an engineer. Maria was educated at home and, in 1940, she went to Leipzig University to study modern languages; by early 1942 she had passed her 'interpreter's diploma' in English and Spanish.

There is no evidence to suggest any of the Molkenteller family were Nazi Party members. However, Maria's father managed to obtain a position for her in a government department in Berlin through a family friend called Mylius. Her mother went with her on that first trip to the capital, and the two women called at the address they had been given just off Nothendarg Platz. Maria was surprised to find the offices guarded by the SS, Hitler's bodyguard, and even more so to find Mylius was an *SS-Sturmbannführer* (major); however, he allayed their fears by saying that the work she would undertake was 'not political'.[2]

In April 1942 Maria began work at the office known as Amt VII of the RSHA, the *Reichsicherheitshauptamt* (Reich Main Security Office), and her ultimate boss was Heinrich Himmler. She worked there for the first six months, spending most of her time reading and translating British and American newspapers. In November 1943, all the departments were moved to 'a hamlet near Glwqau in Silesia' after their offices in Berlin were burned out.[3] It was here she was moved to *Amt* VI for translation work on documents. She worked under a Dr Graefe, who looked after the Turkish section, among others; she was told that the slightest mistake there and she would be discharged.

Over the next six months Maria estimated she translated some 120–150 documents supplied by the commercial attaché, a *sturmbannführer*, at the German Embassy in Ankara. These documents he had obtained, in film form, from the chauffeur of the British ambassador in Turkey, Sir Hughe Knatchbull-Hugessen. The *sturmbannführer* was said to have paid the Turk enormous sums of money, and the films of the documents were exchanged for cash at various meeting places in Ankara.

It was Dr Graefe who told Maria the spy's cover name was 'Cicero'. The documents fell into various categories, eight in total, which she listed and explained for the British in her 'neat hand':

1 The attitude of Turkey towards England and Germany.
2 Preparations for Turkey's entry into the war.
3 Allied conferences at Adana, Teheran and Cairo.
4 Operations 'Overlord', 'Olympia' and 'Saturn'.
5 Economic co-operation of Turkey with England and Germany.
6 Internal Embassy affairs.
7 Sundry matters.
8 Untranslatable material (there was little of this).

Maria indicated several copies were made for various departments, one even going to the Führer himself.

The word 'Overlord' must surely have leapt out at the interrogation officer: what had they known of that? Also, all the minutes of the first and second Cairo conferences are double underlined, maybe by a later reader.[4] Equally there were items of little value, embassy affairs such as the 'List of Christmas boxes 1943' and a report on one of the women staff who was going 'to have an illegitimate child'.[5]

After days of interrogation, which appeared to delight Maria, Captain Basett passed his report, dated 23 May 1945, to his superior Colonel H.L.A. Hart, who then wrote a note on the subject to MI6:

I am sending you now two copies of the interrogation of Maria Molkenteller at Nightingale Lane. You will no doubt look after the Foreign Office interest in this matter, but we would certainly like to know what their comments are after reading this astonishing story.[6]

One can almost hear him laughing and saying, 'My goodness if this gets out we will be a laughing stock'. It was some weeks later in July that the file of one Ludwig Moyzisch would also cross Colonel Herbert Hart's desk.[7]

# 1

# FIRST CONTACT, OCTOBER 1943

The insistent ringing of the telephone brought Ludwig Moyzisch quickly back from the sleep he needed so badly. It was 26 October and he had gone to bed just after ten, reading for a while before switching off the light.

Moyzisch was of slim build, with dark hair; he was a quiet and conscientious man. He was not overly annoyed because the telephone, his line to the outside world, had not been working for days. This happened often in Turkey, and was a point he had discussed with his wife before going to bed.[1]

He was still half asleep when he answered the call: it was Inge Jenke, the wife of Albert Jenke, who was first secretary at the German Embassy.

'Would you please come round to our flat at once? My husband wants to see you.' There was tension in her voice.

Moyzisch asked what the problem was.

'It's urgent. Please come immediately.'[2]

Moyzisch got up and dressed. The call had woken his wife as well, and both felt that, whatever it was, it could probably have waited until morning. However, Inge Jenke was the sister of Joachim Von Ribbentrop, the Reich's Foreign Minister, and she is described as a 'nervous, ambitious woman in her middle forties'. It was therefore wise to humour her.[3]

It was a short drive from where Moyzisch lived to the German Embassy compound in Ankara, known by the Turks as the *Alman Koy*, the German village. The Turkish caretaker opened the gate to allow him in, before Frau Jenke opened the front door of their apartment. She was sorry for having to call him from his bed, and told him that her husband had now retired for the night, but would see him in the morning.

'There's a strange sort of character in there,' she said pointing at the drawing room door. 'He has something he wants to sell us. You're to talk to him and find out what it's all about. And when you go, do please remember to shut the front door after you. I've sent the servants to bed.'[4]

It is odd that, in Moyzisch's account at that time, Inge Jenke did not reveal she knew the character behind the door prior to the visit that night, and that he had worked for the Jenkes, although this fact was revealed to him by the Jenkes the next day.[5] Maybe they did not wish to unduly influence Moyzisch in any way on that first meeting.

Franz Von Papen, the German ambassador, commented:

> The whole business began in a rather puzzling way. Herr Jenke, one of my two ministers, came to me one day to say that a man-servant whom he had employed at one time had rung him on the telephone with an offer to provide us with important information.

At first Von Papen turned down this offer, feeling any spy worth his while would not approach potential employers on the telephone. However, the man first known as Diello by Von Papen '… became insistent, so I gave instructions for Moyzisch to look into the matter'.[6]

Moyzisch entered the room; the curtains were drawn and two table lamps provided light. In an armchair next to one of the lamps sat a man. He got up and spoke in French, asking who Moyzisch was and whether he had been told of his proposition.[7] Moyzisch shook his head and did not reveal his name. The man before him appeared about 50, with thick black hair swept back from a high forehead, already showing signs of balding. His eyes were dark and 'nervous', darting around at every sound in the sleeping house, and below the eyes was a bulbous nose above a firm chin.[8] While the half shadows of the room gave his face a darker complexion, Bazna says he was 38 in April 1943, although Moyzisch never seems to have revised his estimate.[9]

Moyzisch sat down, inviting the man to do the same. Instead, rather theatrically, he went to the door and put his ear to it for a moment, before jerking it open. The hall was empty. He shut the door and returned to his seat. Then, before outlining his proposal, he first insisted Moyzisch should give his word that, whatever the result of their meeting might be, what was said would go no further than his chief. Moyzisch agreed, but, becoming irritated, he made a show of consulting his wristwatch, doubting the man before him had much to offer.

The man took in the gesture and asserted that, once he knew why he was there, he would have plenty of time for him:

I can give you extremely secret papers, the most secret that exist. They come straight from the British Embassy. That would interest you, wouldn't it?

In spying terms, the man was a 'walk-in' – an informant or agent who, without prompting, contacts an intelligence organisation with the offer of information. Moyzisch remained non-committal, still feeling he was dealing with a petty crook.

The man carried on that he would want a lot of money for the documents; after all, he pointed out, the work was extremely 'dangerous'. He wanted 'twenty thousand pounds. English pounds Sterling'. Moyzisch responded that it was 'quite out of the question'. The embassy did not hold such sums of sterling, and the documents would have to be exceptional to command such a price. He would have to see the documents first. Did he have them with him?

'I'm not a fool,' said the man, a superior smile spreading across his face; Moyzisch was annoyed, but remained silent. The man continued by saying that he had spent years preparing for this. They would meet his terms or, he pointed toward the window, he would take the documents to the Soviet Embassy.

'You see I hate the British,' he said.[10]

He then continued to outline his proposal, but still not did not reveal his name. He would give them time to consider his offer, since Moyzisch would need to consult his superiors. He would phone him at 3 p.m. on 30 October in his office and would call himself 'Pierre': if they turned him down, there would be no further contact; if they agreed, he would come and see him at 10 p.m. that same day, at an arranged meeting place, where he would supply two rolls of film of photographed 'Top Secret' British documents, for which they would pay him £20,000. Should they be pleased with what he supplied, they could have more, with each additional film costing them £15,000.

The ball was now in Moyzisch's court, and he was 'inclined' to think the 'offer might be genuine'. They seemed to have little to lose, although it might be a British trick. Moreover, he had doubts his superiors would pay the high price demanded and felt 'the offer would be turned down'. He agreed to what the visitor had outlined and, should the offer be approved, they would meet that night near the gardener's tool shed in the embassy garden, where it was dark and secluded.

At the visitor's request, Moyzisch switched out the lights as he saw the stranger out. As he passed by him, the unknown man gripped his arm and whispered close to his face: 'You'd like to know who I am. I'm the British ambassador's valet.' Thus ended the first meeting.[11]

After leaving the Jenkes' flat, Moyzisch left his car in the embassy compound and walked home. It was a pleasant, cool autumn night, and no doubt he wanted the time to think over what had happened.

The month before he had been in Berlin and had found the capital a grim place. So far it had not suffered greatly in air raids, but the mood was tense and people were apprehensive. The war was going badly: Sicily had fallen, the Allies were now on the Italian mainland, and the situation was critical on the Eastern Front. It would seem that Moyzisch was there for some sort of dressing down. The meeting included those working in foreign embassies for the RSHA, headed by SS *Obergruppenführer* Ernst Kaltenbrunner, under Himmler, and operating under the control of *Amt* VI. Their job was to gather foreign intelligence. Moyzisch's immediate superior was Walter Schellenberg of the *Sicherheitsdienst* (security service), the SD.[12] It was pointed out they had failed to identify the Allied landings in North Africa or the Italian collapse, and their role in the embassies was a waste of time. They had to start supplying good information – 'hot stuff' – and not merely living the good life in foreign cities, or they would be sent to a fighting front.

Just before he left, Moyzisch was given a 'pep talk on all the secret weapons that were being built', and that these would soon restore the fortunes of the Reich. However, he felt such talk would not impress the Turks, and he returned to Ankara full of foreboding for the fate of his homeland.[13]

The Ankara that Moyzisch walked home through on that starlit night had only been capital of Turkey for some twenty years. German and Austrian architects had designed the great boulevards and squares of the city in a Fascist style, while it was the energy of Kemal Ataturk, father of the nation, that had ensured its development.

In the First World War, Ankara had not existed; at that time it was still known by its Byzantine name of Angora, from the Slav word '*gora*'. It was a hill town of a few thousand inhabitants: a poor watering hole on the main road east across Anatolia into Asia; an oasis town on a bone-dry empty plateau, very different from the old capital of Istanbul, influenced so much by the western Greeks. A ruined Byzantine fortress overlooked the town from its hilltop perch. Its only claim to fame had been the famous breed of cat named after it.[14]

It had been known better in ancient times: Alexander the Great had come this way in 333 BC on his way to conquer the known world; he had cut the Gordian Knot nearby. Julius Caesar also paused there in 74 BC. Even before these illustrious visitors, the Hurrians and the Hittites had used the citadel. In 1414 the Ottomans made it part of their empire.[15]

In 1943 Ankara marked the contrast between the old Turkey and the new. A walk along Ataturk Boulevard, the main thoroughfare of the New City, would pass grand embassies, the new buildings of the Turkish Parliament and the various ministries, luxurious hotels, restaurants and well-stocked shops. However, at the end of the street, the walker would enter the old town, taking a market street toward the Citadel, where it is once more an Anatolian town. Winding lanes would be thronged with peasants, dressed in clothing of another time and place, more Asian than European. Here, transport might be a black donkey or a cart; flocks of sheep were still driven through the town to market.

Ankara had a harsh climate: the summers were burning hot, while the snow in winter could be as deep as in his native Austria, and could often be found hanging on into March. Autumn was cool and pleasant but, arriving back home, Moyzisch found everyone asleep: '... but try as I might, I could not get to sleep again myself'.[16]

Moyzisch was well known to his boss in the SD, Walter Schellenberg, who had visited Turkey earlier in 1943. Trade relations between Germany and Turkey had reached a sticky patch over Turkish deliveries of chromium ore to Germany and, as Schellenberg put it: 'I thought that a little pressure might easily put things right. I also intended to carry out an inspection of our secret service organisation in Turkey.'

After arriving in Turkey he was driven to Therapia, where Von Papen had his summer residence. Special envoy Jenke and his wife, Ribbentrop's sister, received him. After three days at Therapia, where he met and talked with Von Papen, he flew to Ankara to have meetings with the Chief of the Turkish Secret Service, which he did together with Moyzisch.[17]

Later, Moyzisch took Schellenberg 'duck-shooting', where he 'had an opportunity of observing the sombre beauties of this rugged and arid country, which looked to me like a lunar landscape.' During his time in Ankara, Schellenberg 'spent a considerable amount of time with Moyzisch's family, to whom he was devoted, and was so impressed by the sincerity and industry with which he tackled his work that I decided to increase his already considerable salary. I instructed him to keep Von Papen informed about his activities, for I felt that a relationship of confidence between them was emphatically necessary.'[18]

# 2

# ELYESA BAZNA

Eric Ambler once wrote dismissively of the idea that chance was a nickname for providence:

> It is one of those convenient, question-begging aphorisms coined to discredit the unpleasant truth that chance plays an important, if not predominant, part in human affairs. Yet it was not entirely inexcusable. Inevitably, chance does occasionally operate with a sort of fumbling coherence readily mistakable for the workings of a self-conscious Providence.[1]

The man that Ludwig Moyzisch met in the Jenkes' flat was Elyesa Bazna. Bazna was born in 1904 from Albanian stock at Pristina, now in Kosovo, then part of the Ottoman Empire. As the Empire shrank, the Bazna family moved to Salonica, where they lived not far from the birthplace of Kemal Ataturk. However, the first Balkan War (1912–13) was a disaster for the Empire and it lost almost all its European territories. Salonika fell to the Greeks, along with the Aegean islands. Ataturk scolded a friend over the city's loss: 'How could you leave Salonica, that beautiful home-town of ours?'[2]

The family moved again, this time to Istanbul, but Elyesa did not settle well at school and was soon expelled. Then, with Turkey finding itself on the losing side of the First World War, Istanbul was occupied by the Allies. He found work with a French transport unit that fuelled his 'passion for cars', but he soon lost that job after wrecking a truck.[3] Various other jobs resulted in more run-ins with the authorities. He may even have been a petty thief at this time, and was known to have stolen a motorbike. He says that once, while arrested by the British, he was beaten and badly treated, and claimed to be some sort of patriot, but later admitted that he simply hated 'ordinary order and discipline'. Finally running afoul of the French occupation forces, he was sentenced to three years in a penal labour camp in France, learning the language in the process.[4]

On his release, he stayed in France and worked for the Berliet vehicle manufacturer, which built trucks for the French Army. He was employed at the Marseilles plant, where he also learned the skills of a locksmith. Finally, he returned to Istanbul where he worked for the city's transport department and fire brigade.

Then, as now, the city of Istanbul was unique: a vast turbulent metropolis which appears beyond control at times. Procopius, court chronicler in the reign of Emperor Justinian the Great, described his beloved city as being surrounded by a garland of waters. The city has changed in the fifteen centuries since he wrote his eulogy of praise for it, even the name (from Constantinople to Istanbul). Yet the waters still flow: the Bosphorus, which travels from the Black Sea to the Sea of Marmara, separates the main European city from its Asian suburbs, and at its southern end the Bosphorus is joined by the Golden Horn. The historic stream which flows seaward from Europe, the left bank of the Golden Horn, is formed from the Levantine port quarter of Galata, and on its right bank is the seven-hilled Imperial City, which some still prefer to call Stamboul.

James Pettifer saw it as:

> … wild, often dissolute, with intersection centres and localities and suburbs, much more a labyrinth than any Greek city. It is the only famous Turkish city, the only place in the country that is not provincial.[5]

Later, with a loan from his father, Bazna bought a Studebaker car and became a taxi-driver. However, he failed to prosper and so became a chauffeur/servant to the Yugoslav ambassador, Jankovic, who he served for seven years. When the capital moved to Ankara, he moved with the diplomatic circle, and was employed as a *kavass*, one who serves foreigners. During this time he married and fathered four children, but his wife and children were in Istanbul, while he was in Ankara. In a few years the couple were estranged and the marriage ended in divorce.

During this period he developed his passion for music. Apparently the ambassador heard him singing while working and advised him he had a good voice and should take lessons to develop it. Finally, after several months of lessons with a German professor of music, he resigned his position to pursue his career in music. He gave a concert in Istanbul at the *Union Française*, the recital based on European opera music, and, although it got good reviews, it was not a success and left him in debt.

He had little choice but to return to his role as a servant. He found employment with the American military attaché, Colonel Class. However, he soon felt sexually attracted to the colonel's wife, who was 'young and pretty', but he knew he meant nothing to her. Bazna felt he might not be able to control his feelings and 'decided that it would be better for me to hand in my notice'.[6]

In late 1942 he was employed by Albert Jenke, then a prominent businessman who had been in Turkey many years and had been appointed to the staff at the German Embassy. In early 1943 Jenke was promoted to minister and assistant to the ambassador, Von Papen. He was the brother-in-law of Von Ribbentrop, German Foreign Minister. Bazna, when talking about his new job, said: 'I did not shrink from poking my nose into my employer's correspondence.'

He went so far as to photograph some documents to show off to his wife. However, he quickly fell under suspicion and found his room had been searched. He was dismissed shortly after by Jenke, who insisted it was for economic reasons. Bazna felt he 'had been taken for a spy'. He did not consider himself one at the time, only that he was being nosey.[7]

Bazna says that it was while he was sitting in the lounge of the Ankara Palace Hotel – drinking coffee and reading the papers in the city's best hotel was a pastime he much enjoyed – that he reviewed his life, which depressed him. He had failed in many things and wondered whether he would be a *kavass* at somebody's beck and call forever. It suddenly struck him like some revelation that he had lost his last job for snooping because 'the Germans had suspected him'. Here among all the warring powers who watched each other, he thought: 'Why not set up as a spy? The idea fascinated me and would not let me go.'

At the same time, his eyes took in an advertisement in the paper, which read: 'Driver wanted for First Secretary of British Embassy.' It seems doubtful that he put these two things together so quickly, as opportunity would surely have been the greatest motive. Nevertheless, that opportunity would soon present itself, for it was not long before he was working for Douglas Busk of the British Embassy.[8]

The interview with Busk was short and Bazna tried to speak mostly in French to questions asked in English. Was this supposed to impress Busk, who had asked him whether he spoke English? He replied he could, but 'only with difficulty'. Busk briefly examined Bazna's references and asked him how he had picked up such good French. He told him that he had lived in Marseilles while working at the Berliet factory. He was asked to write something as a test, which he did in French and seemed to pass easily.

Busk said he would call him by his first name, Elyesa, that the job would require driving, looking after the car and some housework. The wage was 100 Turkish pounds per month, which Bazna felt 'was a very low wage', but, nevertheless, he took the job.[9]

The Busks were expecting a baby, which may have clouded the First Secretary's judgement, in that he was too keen to get help and failed to check Bazna's background. At that time, or shortly afterwards, Mrs Busk was at the American Hospital in Istanbul, where she gave birth to a baby daughter. On her return to Ankara with her daughter, she brought a nursemaid with her, Mara.

Mara was in her thirties and Bazna was soon attracted to her. He described her as 'slender' with 'black hair' and 'bright blue eyes'; she had 'delicate hands and fingers and the graceful way she moved them reminded me of the women of Bucharest'. Did he see something of the gypsy in her? It soon became apparent this attraction was shared, with her 'willingness to be affectionate'. He soon forgot his wife and children in Istanbul and, though he felt disgusted with himself, was in '… a dream world. I quickly fell for Mara.'[10]

He remained working for the Busks for many months. It was most likely that the idea to become a spy came with the opportunities presented at this time. Following his attempt to impress Mara, who he soon convinced that he was working undercover for the Turkish secret police, the *Emniyet*, she became more than willing to help him in his activities. It is not known if Bazna photographed documents while working for the Busks – the First Secretary was meticulous and unlikely to have brought important documents home against the security code – but Bazna did claim to have photographed documents at the Busks' residence, and insisted most of the early films supplied to the Germans came from there.[11]

When it became common knowledge that the ambassador, Sir Hughe Knatchbull-Hugessen, was looking for a valet, Bazna saw his chance. He convinced Mara that he could not keep his hands off her and that a little distance between them would do them both good. She could help him by talking to Mrs Busk and getting her to commend Bazna to the ambassador. It would make their love life more exciting and, above all, they would both be serving the nation.

Douglas Busk took Bazna to see the ambassador with a view to becoming Sir Hughe's valet, as Busk may well have felt he was under-employed in his service anyway. The interview with the ambassador was even shorter than the one Bazna had with Busk, and it appears he was hired largely on his employer's recommendation. Neither Sir Hughe nor Busk had checked his background.

At the start of the interview, Bazna says that Sir Hughe gave Busk a file and asked that he return it in the morning. He was well aware that the Busks were going to a party given by the Soviet commercial attaché. He also claims to have already worked out how to get into Busk's locked desk and briefcase; no doubt his skill as a locksmith was paying dividends.

Taken on straight away, the ambassador's butler, Zeki, showed him around the main residence. His own room was small and on the ground floor, near the kitchen. Sir Hughe's study was on the first floor, above the kitchen. On the second floor were the family bedrooms, and the embassy itself was next door. The butler left him in the ambassador's bedroom to make himself familiar with its layout. In the wardrobe he found dozens of suits and uniforms; in the bedside cabinet he found sleeping pills, which was a 'discovery that gave me pleasure'. There he was discovered by Lady Knatchbull-Hugessen, who briefly questioned him and then left. He felt uncomfortable with her and deduced that he would need to be 'more on my guard with her than with her husband'.

Shortly after, he returned to the Busks' residence to pack his pos-sessions. Mara was more than glad to see him and found 'new ways of demonstrating her affection'. Once the Busks had left for the party with the Soviets, Bazna says he found the briefcase and removed the docu-ments; at the same time helping himself to his master's brandy. Then in the kitchen where he had his Leica camera hidden in one of the sauce-pans, he photographed the documents, page by page, standing on a stool from above. Mara was present throughout. Once finished, he returned the documents to the briefcase and placed it back in the desk drawer. Bazna had no time to read the documents and his English may not have been equal to it anyway; he says that he learnt the contents later on. He started work for the British ambassador the next day.[12]

It is a puzzle just what he supplied to the Germans in the rolls of film on the second meeting with Moyzisch. An MI6 summary went as far as to say that Bazna's account was 'worthless as evidence' unless it could be corroborated elsewhere.[13] However, the conclusion is inescapable that, given Bazna identified the date as 25 October, the night before he appeared at the Jenkes' house, the photographs supplied for sale must have been taken at the Busks' residence. This also clearly demonstrates that, no matter what he said to Moyzisch, he had no real idea of the value of what he had or if he could obtain any more documents. His actions were really those of an opportunist thief.

Yet Bazna also had a degree of skill and cunning in manipulating people. He knew he would 'have to approach them confidently' and it was vital 'that they trust him'. He had taken fifty-two photographs and decided to approach Herr Jenke on 26 October, which he called 'the longest day of my life'.[14]

Why he approached Frau Jenke first, then, is unclear: did he change his mind at some point or was it merely that she answered the telephone? A servant let him into the house, which was next door to the German Embassy on Ataturk Boulevard, after the gate keeper had phoned ahead and cleared his visit. This contradicts Von Papen, however, who says Bazna's first approach was via the telephone to Herr Jenke and he used the name Diello. He rejected the first approach, but Bazna was insistent.

Von Papen regretted not handing the matter to the '*Abwehr* people who worked under the military attaché. But for all I knew the fellow was an *agent provocateur*, and if anyone was going to look foolish, I preferred it to be the Gestapo rather than the *Abwehr*.'[15]

According to Bazna, the Jenkes' servant left him in the drawing room, where he waited a long time smoking. Finally, Frau Jenke came in and told him she did not have much time to spare. He therefore hurriedly outlined his proposal, after which she left the room to fetch her husband. They then both listened closely to what he had to say; he tried to ingratiate himself with them by referring to the bonds of friendship between Turks and Germans. This appeared to annoy Herr Jenke, after which Bazna stuck to the details. Whatever he said was enough to convince them that there could be something worthwhile in his proposal.

Even so, Jenke decided it was not a matter for them, so Frau Jenke made the call that got Moyzisch out of bed. Bazna was left to wait for the man from the SD.[16]

# 3

# BERLIN DECIDES

After his sleepless night, Moyzisch, who had thought of little else but the meeting with the stranger, had gone full circle in his mind:

> I was inclined to revert to my original impression that the man was nothing but a trickster out to put one over the gullible Germans.[1]

However, he had to be careful, for here might be the 'hot stuff' that his superiors were demanding. A bath and coffee put him in a better frame of mind. He concluded that all he really had to do was make a report, others would take the decisions.

Moyzisch arrived early at his office, before his secretary drafted his memo for the ambassador of the night's events. He wondered why the man had approached the Jenkes, but that was discovered after Herr Jenke phoned him and they met again in the Jenkes' flat that morning.

The Jenkes were full of curiosity as to what had happened the night before. Moyzisch told them the strange character 'had a most remarkable offer to make'.[2] It was then the Jenkes told him they had known the man before, but could not remember his name. Yet Bazna tells us that the Jenkes knew exactly who he was, greeting him by his first name, Elyesa.[3] The Jenkes were not surprised to learn that Bazna wanted money, but were surprised that he was demanding such an enormous sum.

It was then that Moyzisch was called to see the ambassador, with Albert Jenke accompanying him. Both men went into Von Papen's office, a large room on the first floor of the embassy. Although Von Papen was in his 60s, he was still handsome, with thin lips, a good head of steel grey hair and sparkling blue eyes.

Franz Von Papen came from an aristocratic Catholic family, and as an army officer he served on the German General Staff before the First World War. He entered the diplomatic service in 1913 and became military attaché to the German ambassador in the United States. He was expelled from the US during the First World War after being accused of espionage and sabotage. Later he served on the Western Front with the 93rd Reserve Infantry Regiment, 4th Guards Infantry Division. He saw action on the Somme in 1916, calling it 'that terrible summer', where his division lost 173 officers and 8,669 men.[4] In 1917 he went to serve with the Ottoman Army in Palestine, which was an experience that equipped him well when he became ambassador to Turkey.

Shortly after the war, Von Papen entered politics, becoming a member of parliament for Prussia. In 1932 he moved centre stage when President Paul Von Hindenburg appointed him chancellor; however, this led to a split with his Centre Party. He was seen as a compromise candidate, though the chaotic nature of politics in Weimar Germany and Von Papen's own fondness for intrigue led to his rapid fall after barely six months when, even with his great charm, he could not command a majority. Thereafter, he tried to gain Nazi support for his government, meeting Adolf Hitler for the first time on 9 June 1932. Von Papen observed:

> I found him curiously unimpressive. Press pictures had conveyed no idea of a dominating personality and I could detect no inner quality which might explain his extraordinary hold on the masses. He was wearing a dark blue suit and seemed the complete petit-bourgeois. He had an unhealthy complexion, and with his little moustache and curious hairstyle had an indefinable bohemian quality.
>
> His demeanour was modest and polite, and although I had heard much about the magnetic quality of his eyes, I do not remember being impressed by them.[5]

Von Papen received no help from Hitler, who told him:

> I regard your cabinet [as] only a temporary solution, and will continue my efforts to make my party the strongest in the country. The chancellorship will then devolve on me.[6]

In the national elections in July 1932, the Nazis gained the biggest share of the vote. They were then the key party and no parliamentary majority could operate without them. In August, Von Papen's government fell and he convinced President Hindenburg that Hitler could be controlled once he was appointed chancellor in a cabinet which was not under Nazi control; and as a check, Von Papen would be vice chancellor of the Reich. Hindenburg finally gave in, appointing Hitler – who he referred to as that 'Austrian Corporal' – chancellor of Germany in January 1933.

Von Papen assured his friends that Hitler 'was his prisoner, tied hand and foot by the conditions he had accepted.' Hitler had the chancellorship, but, in Von Papen's view, the real power rested with the vice chancellor, himself.[7]

Von Papen soon learnt different, since Hitler and the Nazis merely bypassed the cabinet and political convention. Von Papen and the rest of the cabinet were quickly marginalised, so he began to conspire with other conservatives to approach Hindenburg to dismiss Hitler. The growing conflict between the German Army and the Nazi paramilitary arm, the *Sturmabteilung* (SA), led by Ernst Rohm, was the driving force. Ultimately, Von Papen's speech at the University of Marburg on 17 June 1934 led to his downfall, when he called for the end of SA terror in the streets, thus incensing Hitler.

Only two weeks later, Hitler responded to the German Army's demand to suppress the SA and Rohm by purging the leadership. 'The Night of the Long Knives' took place between 30 June and 2 July 1934, in which Rohm and much of the SA leadership were murdered. So, too, were many of the conservatives who opposed Hitler; many of Von Papen's associates were murdered by the SS. Von Papen himself was placed under house arrest on the orders of Hermann Goering, who called it 'protective custody' as it was certain that Von Papen was on the SS death list. Von Papen said:

> I had no doubt that Goebbels, Himmler, and Heydrich had made up their minds that it was time for the Marburg reactionary to be liquidated. I learnt later, the only man who stood between me and this fate was Goering. He probably felt that my liquidation would only complicate matters still more.[8]

Shortly after his release, Von Papen resigned as vice chancellor. As Alan Bullock put it: 'A little late in the day the ex-vice chancellor was beginning to learn he who sups with the Devil needs a very long spoon.'[9]

Despite the widespread murders of 'The Night of the Long Knives', within a month Von Papen had accepted the post of German ambassador in Vienna. He served in that capacity until 1938, and worked toward a peaceful union of the two countries, believing this could only be achieved 'on Austrian initiative.'[10] However, he later admitted: 'Hitler had brought about the *Anschluss* by force, in spite of all warnings and prophecies, his methods had proved the most direct and successful.'[11]

Nevertheless, Von Papen had the satisfaction that: 'When I was relieved of my duties on 4 February [1938], it proved at least that Hitler had realised he would not be able to conduct any policy of aggression with my support.'[12]

Back in Germany, Von Papen retired to his home at Wallerfangen. He was anxious that he would 'be brought to trial on a charge of high treason for having sent to Switzerland the files of his reports to Hitler'.[13] However, nothing came of the matter.

In late 1938, he was offered the post of ambassador in Ankara by Von Ribbentrop, but he declined it. He was offered the post again in February 1939, but again he turned it down. With the coming of the Italian invasion of Albania, again Ribbentrop approached him to take the post in Turkey. Von Papen wrote:

> It was Good Friday, 7 April, 1939, a date I shall always remember. Once again I had to consider whether to assent, against my will, to a post that was to cause me another five years of inner conflict.[14]

He felt the major threat to Turkey was from Fascist Italy, since Mussolini's son-in-law and Italian Foreign Minister, Count Ciano, had been boasting they would station thirty divisions in Albania. It was surmised that *Il Duce* had his eyes on Turkish territories in Europe. In May, Count Ciano met Von Ribbentrop in Berlin; they talked of the 'Turkish Situation'. Ciano wrote in his diary:

> He [Ribbentrop] has been influenced by the suggestions of the superficial Von Papen and so he believes that the Turkish attitude has been determined by fear of Italy.[15]

Reluctantly, Von Papen took the post, but 'I asked to be placed directly under Hitler's orders',[16] and that his work would be outside the domain of the Gestapo. Hitler agreed to these requests, only stipulating that he should work within the framework of the Foreign Office, but he was free at any time to report to Hitler personally on any matter.

In April Von Papen took the Orient Express to Istanbul and, before leaving, he informed Von Ribbentrop that his main aim was 'to keep the peace'.[17] On his arrival, he was soon drawn into the 'Turkish Labyrinth', being greeted with the news that an emissary from Stalin had just arrived in Ankara for talks with the Turkish government. There was no time to enjoy cosmopolitan Istanbul; he hurried east that evening to present himself and his letters of credence to President Ismet Inonu.

The Turks did not welcome the appointment of Von Papen with open arms. They had resisted this choice of German ambassador, as he was too close to Nazi policies and his Machiavellian ways were frowned on. MI6 was well aware of his ability to leave 'entirely false' trails.[18] Indeed, Sir Hughe Knatchbull-Hugessen referred to him as the 'artful dodger'.[19]

However, Von Papen did build up a sizeable group of contacts favourable to his country within the Turkish military and among government officials; in the early years of 1939–41, many Turks saw friendship with Germany as a prudent course to steer. In the longer term, however, the future would be with the western Allies, for early in the war Berlin had concluded pacts with Italy and Russia, earning the distrust of the Turks who saw both countries as potential enemies.

Von Papen was always afflicted by intrigues among the Nazi leaders. Joachim Von Ribbentrop, his superior, hated him and distrusted any information from him, and Von Papen could never be entirely sure what the Jenkes were reporting about his conduct.

In February 1942 Von Papen was almost killed. It was 10 a.m. on one crisp morning, and he and his wife were walking from their house to the German Embassy when an explosion flung them to the ground. The force of the blast broke all the windows in the surrounding buildings. A crowd soon gathered and the Turkish police were quickly on the scene. Von Papen remembered: 'My wife and I made our way to the embassy. Apart from a cut knee and a torn trouser leg, I was unhurt, although my eardrums had suffered from the noise and the force of the explosion. My wife was completely unhurt, but the back of her dress was stained with blood, presumably that of the vanished assailant. Within twenty-four hours the Turkish police had solved the riddle.'[20]

The remains of the hapless bomber were found splattered over the area, including a shoe in a tree. Those responsible were Macedonian students, and another one who was involved in the plot was found to have taken shelter in the Russian Embassy. It was discovered to have been an NKVD operation.[21] However, the controller '… left the Russian Consulate General in Istanbul so speedily that the frontier guards at Erzerum could not be warned soon enough to detain him.'[22]

Von Papen was also being watched by the Nazis; it was even suspected the attack might have been organised by the Gestapo, and the British Secret Service was also in the frame. In the end, Turkish intelligence held the Russians responsible.

'Well gentlemen, what have you been up to?' asked Von Papen of the two men sat before him on an October morning of 1943.

Moyzisch admired the ambassador; Jenke less so, given the influence of the Ribbentrops, but he wanted to safeguard his position should any suspicion fall on him if things went wrong. Moyzisch explained that the night before he had met with the British ambassador's valet. He handed the memo to Von Papen, who read it slowly, glancing over the papers at the two men before him. Finally he finished, laying it on the desk.

'What are we to do, sir?' asked Moyzisch.

Von Papen quickly summed up the situation. The sum requested was too large for them to decide on. He told Moyzisch to draft a signal for Berlin, but to show it to him before sending it. Half an hour later he returned with it to find the ambassador alone. Von Papen read the document, making one or two alterations in his green pencil that only the ambassador used, signed it and handed it back to Moyzisch, asking him to read it out loud.[23]

To the Reich Foreign Minister. Personal. Most Secret.

We have offer of British Embassy Employee alleged to be British Ambassador's Valet to procure photographs of Top Secret original documents. For first delivery on October 30th twenty thousand pounds sterling in bank notes demanded. Fifteen thousand pounds for any further roll of films. Please advise whether offer can be accepted. If so sum required must be despatched by special courier to arrive here not later than October 30th. Alleged Valet was employed several years ago by First Secretary otherwise nothing much known here.

Papen[24]

By the early afternoon of 27 October the decoded signal was on Ribbentrop's desk, who conveyed his annoyance that Jenke had called in Moyzisch of the SD rather than the *Abwehr*. Uncertain what to do, Ribbentrop called in Walther Friedrich Schellenberg for advice.

Schellenberg was head of the foreign intelligence division, and by 1943 had been directly involved in several counter-intelligence operations; he was one of the more free-thinking German intelligence men and an admirer of MI6. He wrote in the *Handbook for the Invasion of Britain:* 'If we really want to understand the structural essence of British Intelligence we must liberate ourselves from conventional ideas.'[25]

On 28 October, Schellenberg met with one of Ribbentrop's personal aides, Horst Wagner, who told him what had happened in Ankara. Schellenberg felt there was little risk involved and acceptance would keep other interested parties, most likely the Russians, out of the frame. Also he 'was pretty sure this case would be handled in Ankara by Moyzisch, and I knew him to be intelligent and experienced.'[26] Ribbentrop decided to use Foreign Office money to keep other departments out of the affair for the time being. Therefore, the first payment was likely to have been in valid currency.

Moyzisch felt sure the proposition would be turned down, saying:

The animosity between the Reich Foreign Minister and the Chancellor of pre-Hitler Germany was unbridgeable, and once Ribbentrop's enmity was aroused it was difficult enough, at the best of times and in most straightforward matters, to get a clear-cut decision out of him. In the circumstances we were all of us practically certain that Berlin would say no.[27]

On 29 October the staff of the German Embassy in Ankara attended the Turkish National Festival; it was also Von Papen's sixty-fourth birthday, so his staff were busy with receptions at the embassy that night. They also had to fit in a reception by the Turkish President at the National Assembly building. Returning in the early afternoon, Moyzisch found a message from the ambassador requesting a meeting. There Von Papen was handed a short decoded signal from Ribbentrop – they had been given the go-ahead.

At 3 p.m. the next day, Bazna telephoned Moyzisch, who thought 'the voice on the other end sounded faint and far away'. He asked if he had the letters.

'Yes,' said Moyzisch.

'I'll see you tonight. *Au revoir.*'[28]

# 4

# SECOND MEETING

Bazna felt the delay until 30 October like a great oppressive weight 'that was almost unbearable'.[1] However, he was busy at the British Embassy, which was active with preparations for the Turkish National Festival. He therefore had to have Sir Hughe's various suits and uniforms ready and in perfect order. At the same time, he was engaged in examining his new position with a view to obtaining a good supply of documents should the Germans take up his offer. He quickly learnt that his master was a creature of habit – a career diplomat of the old school with a regular routine.

At 7.30 a.m. he was called to bring a glass of orange juice. Sir Hughe remained in bed for another thirty minutes reading. On the bedside table was an official black leather box. Sir Hughe then bathed and dressed. He took twenty minutes for breakfast, then went to his study with the black box. Lunch was another twenty-five minutes. After lunch, he usually played the piano for an hour and a half. He had another bath before changing for dinner, which he took with his wife, taking about another thirty minutes.[2]

Bazna had also worked out routes around the house which would be fairly safe for him as a personal servant to use. The ambassador's house was next door to the embassy, which was set in large, well-tended gardens in the Cankaya Hills. He thought it would be best to examine any potential documents when Sir Hughe was away from his study or, better still, not in the house. He could use one of two staircases to take documents to his own room for photographing:

My room, in the servant's quarters, was small and simply furnished. It contained a bed, a cupboard, a table and chair.

I supplemented this by buying a 100-watt bulb for the bedside lamp. I also bought four metal rods and a metal ring. I could screw my camera to the ring, and the metal rods could be used to support the ring.

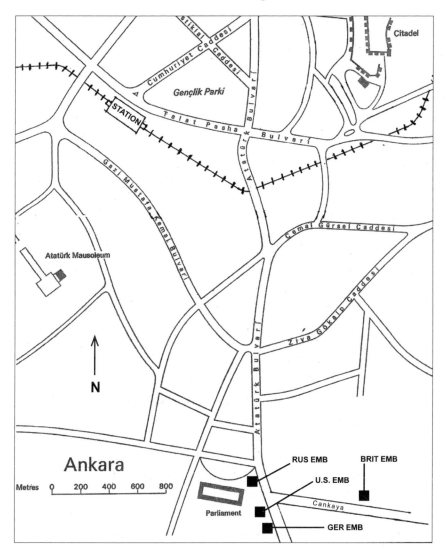

Ankara city centre.

Thus I had a 'tripod' I could use for photographing documents; all I had to do was lay them between the metal rods. I also devised subsidiary uses for the rods and rings to divert suspicion from their real purpose.[3]

The next day, Bazna took the afternoon off. He met Mara in the town on Ataturk Boulevard; they strolled and window-shopped in the autumn sunshine. It was at 3 p.m. that he was due to call Moyzisch. He told her he had already taken photographs of documents at the embassy, as he had quickly established the routine attached to the red and black official boxes, and the whereabouts of the safe key at various times. During the day it was kept in the office of the ambassador's private secretary, Louise, and she took charge of it. At night the ambassador kept it along with the keys to any red and black boxes he had.

Bazna went on to tell Mara that he had taken impressions of several keys with wax and now had the duplicates. She admired his nerve. However, was this mere bravado to impress her? There is some doubt when he did obtain copies; he indicates that a locksmith in the Istanbul Municipal Transport Department made them for him.[4] Was this possible after he had only been working at the embassy for a few days? Also, Moyzisch later claimed that he obtained the duplicate keys for Bazna:

> He wanted to know if his lump of cobbler's wax had been sent to Berlin. He needed those keys urgently. They would enable him to do his photographing while his chief was away from the embassy. He would feel much safer working that way.[5]

Bazna says he was delayed in making the phone call to Moyzisch by a chance meeting with Manoli Filoti, the chef at the embassy, who was much taken with Mara and began 'eagerly discussing recipes' with her.[6] Finally, he left them to it and hurried to the phone booth. By the time he was dialling the number, Bazna was in a cold sweat. He gave Moyzisch the codename 'Pierre' and was informed the meeting was on.

After Bazna's call, Moyzisch reported to Von Papen to confirm the meeting was due that night at 10 p.m. The ambassador warned him not to be taken in by the man he referred to as Diello, although he knew he was called Elyesa from the Jenkes.[7] He also reminded Moyzisch he would be on his own if anything should go wrong.

Moyzisch impressed on Von Papen that he would hand over no money until he had checked and was satisfied with the material. The ambassador handed over a large bundle of sterling banknotes, consisting of ten-, twenty- and fifty-pound notes in bundles. Moyzisch felt they were 'suspiciously new'.[8] Von Papen agreed, but there was nothing they could do. He counted the money, then wrapped it in the large front page of the newspaper *La Republique*. Returning to his own office, he locked the money in his safe.

Bazna returned to the British Embassy in time to lay out Sir Hughe's dinner jacket for the evening. During this time, he went to the ambassador's room and removed the documents from the boxes he found there, taking them below stairs to his own room.

There he quickly set up his photographic equipment using the 100-watt lamp and photographed them all in only three minutes. He then hurried back to Sir Hughe's room to find the door ajar and the ambassador inside talking on the telephone. Gripped by panic, he remained in the corridor outside. However, he heard the door closing and turned away as if heading in the opposite direction; Sir Hughe hurried past him without a word, heading for the dining room. Once Sir Hughe had disappeared, Bazna turned back to the room and replaced all the documents in their boxes in the correct order. However, later that night he decided not to take that roll of film with him: 'That roll of film had nearly brought me disaster. I was not going to risk my neck with it twice in one evening.'[9]

Just before 10 p.m., Moyzisch was waiting near the tool shed by the fence in the embassy garden. The night was dark and still; it was cold and the sky was illuminated by stars. Bazna had already climbed through a hole in the wire fence and was watching in the shadows until he was sure Moyzisch was alone. The SD man finally called out softly.

Bazna replied, 'It's me, Pierre.'[10] His voice and its closeness startled Moyzisch.

They walked in silence to the embassy, where there were no lights on in that part of the building. In his room, where the curtains were drawn, Moyzisch switched on the light, momentarily blinding them both. Neither man showed mutual trust, with both asking to see what they had for the other: Bazna took out the two rolls of 35mm film, while the SD man counted the money he had taken from the safe, and then asked for the rolls of film. Bazna handed them over, expecting the money in return.

'Not yet,' said Moyzisch. He could only have it once the films had been checked; it would only take fifteen minutes. He returned the money to the safe and then left the office for the darkroom, locking Bazna in, for fear that the caretaker might stumble upon him on his rounds. Moyzisch had a photographer waiting for him in the darkroom:

He had made all the necessary preparations. The developer was ready and brought to the correct temperature. He put both the films in the developing tanks. I asked him to explain all his actions to me in detail, because in future I intended to do all this myself. It took much longer than I expected.[11]

Finally, in spite of the small negatives, he could confirm they were documents. With a magnifying glass he could read clearly 'Most Secret, from Foreign Office to British Embassy, Angora' and a receipt date. He returned to his room, after locking the darkroom and asking the photographer to return shortly. Bazna seemed at ease, with only the full ashtray marking the passing of time.

Moyzisch handed over the money and tried to get a signed receipt. Bazna thought 'my ears had deceived me, but then I burst out laughing'. Moyzisch grinned and confessed to being too much the bureaucrat.[12]

Bazna accepted a glass of whisky and the two men drank to each other's health. The spy then asked if the Germans could supply him with a better camera, a Leica, more film and a revolver. Moyzisch questioned the need for the revolver, but finally agreed to get one for him, although he had offered no explanation for the request. They arranged to meet the next night at the same time and place, despite the fact that Moyzisch had no more money readily available. Bazna replied that he would extend credit to the Germans, before leaving the embassy by the route he had come.

Moyzisch spent the rest of the night printing the pictures from fifty-two photographs. The photographer gave him instructions on producing enlargements, then left him in the dark room alone. He concentrated first on finishing the pictures, which he found 'clear and perfectly exposed and easily legible'.[13] It took him until 4 a.m. to finish. He disposed of all duplicates and spoiled enlargements from the developing process by ripping them up and flushing them down the toilet. Then he returned to his room with the films and enlargements, where he locked himself in and studied the images. The value of the information became apparent immediately: none of the documents were more than fourteen days old; most were signals between the Foreign Office in London and the embassy in Ankara, though some were exchanges between London, Washington and Moscow; and all were marked 'Top Secret' or 'Most Secret'.[14] Finally, Moyzisch fell asleep at his desk as dawn broke.

# 5

# THEY CALLED HIM CICERO

Moyzisch was awoken by his secretary, 'Schnurchen', banging on the locked door at 9 a.m. the next morning. The shock made him wake with a start, knocking some of the photographs on the floor. Soon he was waiting, tired, dishevelled and unshaven, in the ambassador's ante-room under the disapproving gaze of Fraulein Rose, the ambassador's long-standing secretary. He started looking at the photographs to divert attention. She asked him what he had: 'Just some nudes, the bare facts one might say,' he replied, before he was accused of being 'coarse'. Suddenly Moyzisch realised there were only fifty-one photographs. He asked Rose to count them, but she also came to fifty-one – he had lost one:

> I grabbed the folder of photographs, put it under my arm, tore open the door, and ran downstairs. At the front door I almost crashed into the Ambassador, who was coming in. I did not stop or say a word. As I jumped past him, down the last three steps, I had a fleeting impression of Herr Von Papen's expression. He was looking at me as though I had gone mad.[1]

Moyzisch found the missing photograph lying face down near the main gate. He went back to his room, where he took a glass of water from his secretary to calm down, before returning to see the ambassador. Von Papen says nothing of this other than Moyzisch was 'pale and unshaven'.[2] Some observers have been inclined to question Moyzisch's account,[3] although Dick White of MI5 found Moyzisch's book, *Operation Cicero*, to be reasonably authentic.[4]

When studying the photographs, Von Papen surmised that Moyzisch's grasp of English was not sufficient for him to fully understand the importance of the documents. The ambassador soon 'realised that we had come upon a priceless source of information'.[5] Later the SD man admitted that, after his long sleepless night, he found it difficult to concentrate on what Von Papen was saying or even to stay awake during the meeting.[6] He also concluded that they could not continue with 'Pierre' as a codename for the spy, particularly when dealing with higher authority in Berlin. The name Pierre was: 'Very unimaginative. We've got to give him a codename that even he doesn't know. How about this: since his documents are so very, very eloquent, let's call him Cicero.'[7]

Bazna claimed to the contrary, even saying he called his house in Ankara Cicero Villa.[8] However, it is fairly certain he knew nothing of his codename until Moyzisch's account was released in the 1950s.[9] It is also highly unlikely, as he claims, that he took Mara on a spending spree shortly after that meeting. There would hardly have been time, and he had already been embarrassed by bumping into the chef from the British Embassy. Moreover, Ankara at the time was a hotbed of intrigue, with agents from many nations. Yet, he says they went to the ABC store on Ataturk Boulevard, '... the smartest store in Ankara', where he bought Mara '... expensive scent, luxurious underwear, and whisky'.[10] He was concerned and nauseated with the amount she drank, but at the same time bewitched by her when she was drunk.

He rented a house in the Kavaklidere hills in the Cankaya district of the city, which was well south of the British Embassy but closer to the German Embassy along the Cankaya–Caddesi road. However, he did not keep his money there; he could not bring himself to trust Mara, preferring instead to hide it under the carpet of his room at the British Embassy.

The night of the second meeting, Moyzisch and Cicero met again at the tool shed in the embassy garden at 10 p.m. Again Cicero was there first and, after exchanging pleasantries, he asked if they had found the goods satisfactory. Moyzisch confirmed that they had.

They once again went to Moyzisch's office and locked themselves in. Cicero went through his routine of checking the room by moving the long curtains and searching for eavesdroppers, while the SD man sat at his desk, amused by these actions. Finally, Cicero sat down and helped himself to whisky from the decanter on the desk. He then placed two rolls of 35mm film in front of Moyzisch, who locked them away in his desk drawer. Cicero was happy enough to wait for payment of £30,000 until their next meeting.

They drank to each other's health. Moyzisch tried to question Cicero on his photography techniques, praising his skill and asking if he had an assistant. Cicero avoided any direct answer, again asking for a new camera, which he advised them to send direct from Germany. Cicero says Moyzisch gave him a revolver at this meeting.

It was close to midnight before Cicero left. He told Moyzisch he would ring him to arrange the next meeting, but felt it was risky to continue their meetings at the embassy, as it was likely to be under surveillance. He suggested they meet in the old part of the city, in a dark street.

'You've got a car, I suppose?' asked Cicero.

Moyzisch confirmed that he did.[11]

They arranged the meeting place that night. Somewhere he could drive slowly and Cicero might jump in, although if there was anybody about Moyzisch could ignore him and drive around the block. The Mercedes the SD man usually drove was in the garage for repair, so he borrowed the car of a friend. The powerful Opel Admiral looked like an American model; many such cars were seen around Ankara and were used by the German diplomatic corps and by the Turkish government.

A few days later, Moyzisch bought the car to use for his rendezvous with Cicero, while 'by day I continued to drive the old Mercedes, which everyone in Ankara knew to be mine'.[12]

Cicero hid in the back of the Opel Admiral and directed Moyzisch through the back streets, finally pointing out a piece of wasteland between two houses where he was to pick him up. They also agreed on a new telephone code, whereby the meeting time would be twenty-four hours earlier than the time and date mentioned over the telephone.

Then Cicero asked to be driven to the British Embassy at Cankaya. Moyzisch was shocked at this request, but complied, although, as they neared the embassy, it crossed his mind it might be a trap. Cicero asked him to slow to a crawl but not stop, and then with a gentle click of the back door he was gone.

A few minutes later, Moyzisch parked the Opel back at the German Embassy. The only light came from the Jenkes' flat, who he knew were having a small party. He went to the darkroom and developed the two new rolls of film, which produced forty exposures. He left them to dry and then joined the Jenkes' party. There he drank some strong coffee and watched some guests playing poker at two tables. When the Japanese ambassador left, he took his place at the table for a few hands, but found it difficult to concentrate. The party broke up at 3 a.m. and he returned to the darkroom to make the enlargements; once again it was dawn by the time he had finished.[13]

He studied them for a while, then locked them in the safe and went home to bed for two and a half hours, leaving instructions to be called at 11 a.m. About midday he was at the ambassador's office with the fresh photographs. The documents covered the first minutes of the third Moscow Conference, which was still going on, hosted by Soviet Foreign Minister Vyacheslav Molotov and attended by British Foreign Secretary Anthony Eden and the US Secretary of State, Cordell Hull.

# 6

# WHO IS CICERO?

The various intelligence departments in Berlin had begun to badger Moyzisch for details on Cicero. Who was this man? What was his background? What motivated him? They were concerned they might lose him, as Moyzisch observed:

> It was particularly Kaltenbrunner, newly appointed chief of the Nachrichtendienst, which was that part of the German Secret Service not controlled by the Foreign Ministry, who began to take an unpleasantly personal interest in Operation Cicero. Day after day we were inundated with signals from various members of his large staff.[1]

Cicero phoned again the next day, inviting Moyzisch to play bridge at 9 p.m. on 6 November. Moyzisch was out of the office and his secretary took the message. So, the next delivery would be made that night. He almost missed the meeting when the Opel refused to start, but after a few minutes he got the car going and set off quickly with dirty hands. Even so, he was a few minutes late.

Cicero flashed him with a torch, which Moyzisch found an 'unnecessary signal' and unlike the man to draw attention to himself.[2] However, Cicero may have thought he was having trouble finding him, as Moyzisch admitted he was running late. Cicero got in, they exchanged the film for £30,000, and he stuffed the bundle of banknotes under his overcoat. Moyzisch kept driving; he tried to question Cicero, explaining Berlin wanted to know more about him.

Cicero told him that was none of his or Berlin's business; however, vanity got the better of him, telling him, 'I'm no Turk, I'm an Albanian'.[3] He also told him his father had been shot by an Englishman. Little else passed between them before Cicero asked him to slow down and, with a click of the door, he was gone into the night.

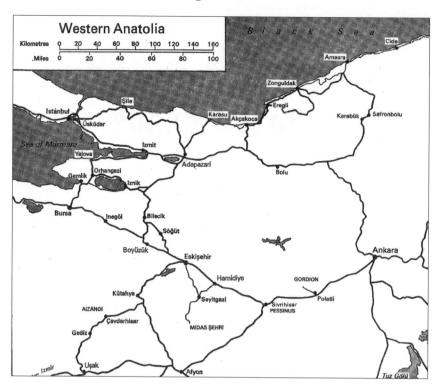

Western Anatolia.

Back at the German Embassy, Moyzisch developed twenty pictures of documents, all marked 'Top Secret'. At this point, he was getting more efficient and finished the job by 2 a.m. He saw Von Papen the next morning, who had a signal from Berlin signed by Von Steengracht, Under Secretary at the Foreign Ministry: Moyzisch was to go to Berlin and see the minister, and was to bring all the Cicero material with him.

In the new documents was a full account of the Casablanca Conference, which had taken place in January 1943. It was fairly old material, but it was the first time that Von Papen had heard the phrase 'unconditional surrender' – a term first suggested by President Roosevelt, but which was to prove 'a fatal stumbling block' for the Nazis and the German people.[4]

Von Papen also noted Churchill's idea to invite the Turks to enter the war, and that he had tried to arrange a meeting with the Turkish leaders on the island of Cyprus. However, in further correspondence it soon became apparent that Turkey feared Russia, her old enemy, more than

Germany. Indeed, even on the British Crown Colony of Cyprus, the Turkish-Cypriots tended to back the Germans.[5] An SOE officer assessed the situation as: 'The Turks influenced by their *Hodjas* [leaders] continue to remain pro-German. This was reported to me from agents in Paphos and Limassol.'[6]

A seat was booked for Moyzisch on a Junkers 52 courier plane leaving Istanbul the next morning. To catch it he needed to take the night Anatolian Express to Istanbul. German diplomats carrying official documents were supposed to travel in a first-class compartment alone, but the train was full and Moyzisch had to make do with a second-class compartment, which he shared with what he took to be an Englishman. He spent a restless night as, conscious of what he was carrying, he didn't trust the stranger. However, they seemed to tolerate one another with guarded affability, and his travelling companion left the train at Haydarpaşa. At Istanbul he was taken straight out to the airport where the aircraft was waiting for him, and he managed to catch up on some sleep during the flight.

The Ju 52 took him to Sofia, where it was due to refuel for the onward journey, and here Moyzisch was summoned over the loudspeaker system in the terminal building; at the information desk he was informed that a special plane was waiting for him and ready to take off, on the instructions of SS General Kaltenbrunner, which would take him straight to Berlin. He 'wondered what was the sudden urgency to see the Cicero documents'[7] and was filled with apprehension, yearning to return to the congenial atmosphere of Ankara.

An icy wind was blowing when he landed at Tempelhof Airport in Berlin and there was snow on the ground. He was picked up by a car that took him to 101 Wihelmstrasse, headquarters of the *Reichsicherheitshauptamt*, the RSHA, central security office. He was told that Kaltenbrunner wanted to see the documents before Ribbentrop, and it became clear that he was walking into the on-going bitter feud between the two men.

In September 1939, a major consolidation took place of the SS police and intelligence operations: the SD main office and Security Police main office were amalgamated to become RSHA (Reich Security Main Office).[8] There were two reasons concerning the SD main office: first, to rationalise and streamline the systems. Back in 1937, the Gestapo was made the sole state security investigative agency, which made the SD redundant. However, it could conduct operations abroad, although generally it proved pretty poor in doing so compared with the *Abwehr*, the armed forces intelligence service, headed by Admiral Wilhelm Canaris. Second, the SD was a party formation and funded by the Nazi Party. The architect of the merger was Walther Schellenberg, who had joined the SS in 1933 and rose quickly through the ranks as a protégé of Reinhard Heydrich. He sought to bring the SD within the state fold and ensure it would be adequately resourced.[9] By the time of Operation Cicero, therefore, the SD was on the way to taking over the *Abwehr*, and Canaris would shortly fall from power and be confined to house arrest.

Moyzisch was met at the entrance of the RSHA by two men and led through the labyrinthine corridors of the building, before arriving at the office of Kaltenbrunner, the new chief of the SS Secret Service, who had recently succeeded Himmler after the death of Reinhard Heydrich. He had been senior SS and Police Leader Danube, based in Vienna, and, like Moyzisch, was an Austrian by birth.[10] His face was covered in duelling scars, and he had a deep booming voice to match his bulky frame.

Once the documents from Ankara were laid out, Kaltenbrunner handed them over to the four other men in the room, who were experts and would examine them to ascertain if they were genuine. Moyzisch then proceeded to tell them of the details of Operation Cicero, for Kaltenbrunner feared it was 'still possible the whole thing might be a cunning trap laid by the enemy'.[11] One of the four men plugged in a tape recorder, then they questioned him. After an hour, Moyzisch asked for a break, after which they continued for another hour. The rolls of film had been taken to a laboratory and examined in minute detail.

At last the experts were finished and dismissed, then the interview 'became less formal.' They sat in more comfortable armchairs and the general told him that, as he knew, Ribbentrop loathed Von Papen and, as far as he was concerned, Moyzisch was one of the ambassador's men. Operation Cicero was entirely Moyzisch's department's business. Ribbentrop was already convinced Cicero was a British plant, but Kaltenbrunner would talk to the Führer and the matter would 'be handled entirely by this department. So in future you'll take your instructions from me and from nobody else.'[12] He told him the £200,000 had come from his department.

Moyzisch admitted Operation Cicero was a great strain on him, and he was not helped by a constant stream of messages from various departments. Kaltenbrunner went on to ask more questions about Cicero, and Moyzisch reiterated his belief that Cicero was genuine; surely it was more certain after he had confided to him that his father was shot by an Englishman.

Kaltenbrunner exploded in fury at this, saying this was the first he had heard of it. Moyzisch said he had reported the matter, it being sent in the diplomatic bag to the Foreign Ministry. Surely this must have come up in the two hours of questioning, but apparently not. It left Kaltenbrunner even more furious, for he had been duped by Ribbentrop; he leapt to his feet and paced the room. Returning to the desk he banged on it with a clenched fist, saying Ribbentrop was a cheat and a scoundrel, before quickly regaining his self-control.

Kaltenbrunner told Moyzisch that he had been informed that Sir Hughe Knatchbull-Hugessen was 'an excellent diplomat' and 'conscientious', and a great expert on the Middle East. For him to be in Ankara proved the importance the British ascribed to Turkey. 'As for your future reports on Operation Cicero, you'll receive my personal instructions when you get back to Ankara. When are you leaving by the way?'[13]

Moyzisch was unsure as it depended on Ribbentrop, since it was he who had summoned him to Berlin. He asked the general to ring Ribbentrop to make his appointment, and it was agreed that the minister would see him at 7 p.m. the following evening. All the Cicero documents were left with Kaltenbrunner for safekeeping, and Moyzisch was escorted to the door. Kaltenbrunner finished with the words: 'Good luck to you. You'll need it. And remember your future reports, every word of them, are liable to be of the utmost importance to Germany.'[14]

From the start, the Cicero documents had more than one destination in Berlin. Important embassy matters went out by signal, but more physical matters went in the diplomatic bag on the regular courier plane. The constant questions Moyzisch complained about came mainly from SD headquarters, where Walther Schellenberg compiled all the material for his memoranda and briefing for Kaltenbrunner; he had voiced his concerns to the right person. Himmler was also kept aware, and he in turn could decide what Hitler needed to see. It was left to the SD technicians to scrutinise every piece of material for deception, and cryptanalysts to use the information to work on breaking British codes.[15]

Von Papen's material went to the Foreign Ministry and found its way to Ribbentrop's desk, who felt it was his role to present the material to Hitler, as most of the Cicero papers were in the realm of foreign policy and he had agreed with Himmler to deal with political information.

However, the SD was under the orders of the Führer to send reports direct to him, and this conundrum was left to fester, adding more mistrust between the various departments.

The meeting at the Foreign Ministry the next evening was not attended by Ribbentrop. Moyzisch was interviewed by two senior Foreign Ministry officials, Moyland Von Steengracht and Gunther Von Altenburg, while two SD men who had delivered the documents to Moyzisch for the meeting remained with him throughout. Both officials seemed quickly convinced that the documents were genuine. Von Steengracht commented that Cicero must be a 'remarkable fellow'.

Moyzisch said, 'His determination is enormous, and, from what I've seen of him so far, he seems uncommonly intelligent and careful.'

'So you believe in him?' said Von Altenburg. 'You exclude the possibility that he has been planted on us by the British?'

'I do, but I can't prove it. Not yet, at any rate,' replied Moyzisch honestly.

'There's nothing else you can tell us?' asked Von Altenburg.

Moyzisch shook his head.

The two officials got up, bringing the interview to an end. Von Steengracht glanced at the two SD men, and said, 'The Foreign Minister regrets he cannot see you himself today. The documents and the rolls of film will stay here. You are to remain available to be at the Minister's disposal. I suppose we can reach you at the Kaiserhof at any time?'

The two 'bulldogs', as Moyzisch called the SD guards, escorted him to his hotel where he 'stayed, alone with my thoughts'.[16]

Two days later, Moyzisch received an urgent message from Rudolf Likus, an old friend of his at the Foreign Office, to come and see him at No. 16 Behrenstrasse, an annex of the Foreign Ministry. When he got there he was told it was imperative that the minister see him. On the drive to the ministry, Likus told him Ribbentrop was in a temper and furious with Kaltenbrunner, and he was convinced the whole Cicero thing was a British trick. He went on to advise him to humour the minister, even agree with him, and try if possible to avoid mentioning Von Papen. Ribbentrop had also not forgiven Moyzisch for his role in the Spellman Incident.

The Spellman Incident had taken place early in May 1943, when the New York Archbishop Francis Spellman had visited the Levant. Von Papen had felt there was an opportunity to open a link to the US government, with a view to obtaining terms for a negotiated peace for an increasingly isolated Germany. However, Ribbentrop had rejected such an approach. Von Papen tried again, with Moyzisch acting as intermediary, and arranged for a German Catholic lawyer and scholar to meet with the archbishop. However, Ribbentrop got wind of what was going on and quickly put a stop to it. Moyzisch may have overdramatised it, saying he was '… kept on tenterhooks for a considerable time as to whether or not I was to be recalled to Germany to face a treason trial, and probably a firing-squad'.[17]

However, Von Papen doesn't give great weight to the incident, saying Ribbentrop had 'given a second flat refusal to any idea of such a contact and I was unable to arrange for any conversation with the Cardinal'.[18]

After walking through innumerable corridors within the ministry, Moyzisch and Likus reached Ribbentrop's office. Moyzisch had not seen Ribbentrop for some time, and thought him 'much aged'. He got up when they came in, but remained behind his desk, arms folded, cold blue eyes fixed on the visitors. Moyzisch found the long silence 'oppressive', despite Likus attempting to break the ice with some small talk. They all sat around a table where the Cicero documents were spread out. Ribbentrop idly played with them, spreading them out like cards, then, tidying the pile, he began to talk.

'So you have met this Cicero, what sort of man is he?'

Once again Moyzisch went through what he knew. Ribbentrop remained caustic, pointing out that the man was only interested in money. All he really wanted to know was whether the documents were genuine.

'My personal opinion …' began Moyzisch.

'I'm not interested in your personal opinions,' retorted Ribbentrop. 'What does Jenke think?'

Moyzisch said Jenke agreed with him, as did Von Papen. He soon realised his mistake in mentioning the ambassador's name, but it was too late. Ribbentrop became even colder in tone. Likus shot Moyzisch a look of despair. Ribbentrop spoke again, saying he needed facts not opinions, and wondered if Moyzisch was really up to the job: 'Or shall I send someone else to Ankara?'

Silence briefly descended. Likus spoke up, pointing out that it must be a difficult job for Moyzisch, and that it would be better to concentrate on finding out if Cicero worked alone. If indeed he did, he reasoned it would go a long way to confirming the papers were genuine. Ribbentrop agreed.

'You are to stay in Berlin for the time being,' said Ribbentrop. 'I may want to see you again.'

'But sir,' pointed out Moyzisch, 'Cicero is waiting for me in Ankara, with new documents.'

'You are to stay in Berlin for the time being,' repeated the minister.

There was no further argument from Moyzisch.[19]

Schellenberg met Moyzisch the next day, and conveyed his annoyance that his man had been ordered to Berlin at the whim of Ribbentrop, He had complained to Kaltenbrunner about Ribbentrop's intervention in the case. At the meeting he generally agreed with Moyzisch's handling of Cicero, and told him he 'believed the material was genuine'.[20]

He went on to give Moyzisch fresh instructions:

… that all rolls of film brought to him by 'Cicero' should be sent to Berlin at once, so that our technicians could make the required number of copies for distribution to the interested authorities. If Moyzisch needed technical assistance, it could be sent out on the twice-weekly courier planes. A technician, with all the necessary equipment for a modern photographic laboratory, was to be sent to Ankara at once under diplomatic immunity.[21]

Soon after his meetings with Ribbentrop and Schellenberg, Moyzisch began to get social invitations to meet people as if he were some sort of celebrity. Two were from the notable exile, Rashid Ali el-Gailani, the former pro-Axis Iraqi premier, who had fled his country after a failed bid to throw out the British; he got limited help and was sold down the river, Mussolini considering Axis support as only symbolic.[22] In August 1940, Von Papen had tried to help the Axis factions in Iraq by meeting various people in Ankara, where he was led to believe the Grand Mufti was coordinating action.[23] The German-Egyptian spy, Johannes Eppler, met the Grand Mufti in Baghdad, trying to assess the situation; he called him 'the world champion of intrigue' and that he was 'vulgar and tasteless'.[24]

Moyzisch had met Rashid Ali before, and spent an 'enjoyable evening' with him. A few days later he met the Grand Mufti, who he felt 'overestimated my importance'. However, he did confide to him he felt the Third Reich was doomed: the 'idea' had failed and was coming to 'a violent and terrible end'.[25]

On this round of visits he also saw the Japanese ambassador, Hiroshi Oshima, who congratulated him on his success. It appeared that he, too, had knowledge of Operation Cicero. It put Moyzisch in a bad frame of mind, and he began to wonder how many people in Berlin now knew about Cicero. Certainly many within the highest official circles did. Joseph Goebbels wrote in his diary for 13 November: 'I have received confidential information which enables me to appraise the Moscow Conference.' His appraisal was from the Western Allies' point of view, and he was glad to see no accord had been reached between Britain and Turkey over the use of air bases. There is little doubt where the information had come from.[26]

By the time Moyzisch was the toast of Berlin, Hitler already knew about Cicero from Von Papen. The ambassador had flown to Berlin after it became apparent, he believed, that the Turks 'were prepared to declare war under the final threat of British political and economic pressure'. While at the Führer's headquarters, he 'also gave details of a new source of information which was to prove of the greatest possible value to us in the coming months'.[27]

On the morning of 22 November, the Foreign Minister ordered Moyzisch to return to Ankara. He had seen nothing of Ribbentrop during the two weeks of waiting: 'The official business that I had transacted during that time could easily have been completed in one day'.

He left Berlin that night via the Berlin–Breslau–Vienna express. Moyzisch noted that the train left before the 'scheduled time' and did not stop at the Berlin suburb stations. Later he learned the reason: a heavy force of British bombers was approaching the city.[28] Von Papen was caught in one of these raids at about this time:

In Berlin I experienced at first hand the full horror of the raids. During one of the worst attacks I was sitting with my son and daughters in the cellar of our house. Everything in the neighbourhood was reduced to rubble, and although we managed to put out incendiary bombs which had fallen through into my study, the house became uninhabitable, with its doors and windows blown out and roof destroyed.

The next morning Von Papen found:

… practically the whole of the Wilhelmstrasse … including the Foreign Office lay in ruins.

All the railway stations had been severely damaged and no one could tell me whether it would be possible to start my return journey that afternoon. We waited on the station platform from midday onwards, and then towards evening the air-raid alarm sounded again. The crowd of would-be travellers made no attempt to seek shelter and in the middle of the raid a train made its way into the station in complete darkness.[29]

When Moyzisch left Berlin that night by train, he wasn't to know that he would not see the city again until the end of the war.

# 7

# AROUND ANKARA

By the time the Ju 52 landed at Yedilkay Istanbul airport, it was far too late for Moyzisch to catch the night train to Ankara. He was glad to see the city after the chaos of Berlin and be able to take a short break; he had the evening and the next day free. Cicero could wait.

He caught the night train from Haydarpaşa Station the next evening, which has an inscription near the door 'recording the activities of Lawrence of Arabia in old Scutari'.[1] Not far away, near Uskudar, stood the large barracks of Scutari, used as a hospital for wounded British troops from the Crimean War, and then as a prison for Turkish radicals.

It was growing dark by the time the train left the shore of the Bosphorus. It took sixteen hours to cross the wide expanses of the Anatolian Plain. Moyzisch slept well on the train, and next day relaxed and enjoyed watching the countryside roll by. Ten minutes after arriving in Ankara he was back home, where his secretary told him 'Pierre' had phoned several times. With this, he went straight to see the ambassador, who Moyzisch says 'wanted all the news from Berlin'.[2] An odd request given that Von Papen had been in the capital at about the same time. He was not pleased by all the rumours and chatter about Cicero, and believed 'the gossiping idiots will land us in a first class row here in Ankara yet'.[3] He was also incensed by Kaltenbrunner's demand that all material about Cicero went to him directly: 'Tell your superiors that as long as I am ambassador here in Ankara, I refuse to tolerate such a procedure. You are my subordinate, and I require you to show me in the first instance all the material that passes through your hand.' He intended to evaluate any political material, whatever Ribbentrop or Kaltenbrunner said. After the war, Von Papen found out that he had not 'been allowed to see the whole material, and that some of it must have been sent direct to Kaltenbrunner'.[4]

Cicero rang again that afternoon and they fixed the meeting time for 9 p.m. that evening. Moyzisch does not indicate if they were still using their agreed code, although we can assume that they were.[5]

Moyzisch arrived at the meeting place on time, but there was no sign of Cicero. So he drove around the block twice, before he saw him signalling with his torch. Once in the car, Cicero seemed happy, saying he had missed their meetings and asking where he had been. Moyzisch explained his absence in Berlin was on account of his passenger, which Cicero evidently enjoyed.

Cicero told Moyzisch he had done a few jobs while he was away, but had exposed one roll of film when he had been unable to contact him, for he was worried about carrying it. Yet he still expected payment; he was informed that Berlin would never sanction payment for blank films.

That night Moyzisch drove him to a room in a friend's house, which he had borrowed for the evening where they could relax, and there he paid Cicero the £15,000 still owed. While Cicero handed over two new rolls of film, putting them on the table, again he tried to deliver a third – the spoiled film – but Moyzisch refused, placing it back into Cicero's coat pocket where he touched the hard surface of the revolver.

Again Moyzisch brought the conversation around to Cicero's background as they ate the sandwiches and drank the wine he had provided, hoping the convivial atmosphere might loosen Cicero's tongue. He told him he had been instructed to ask these questions in Berlin, and to find out more about his father's death.

'I don't like talking about it,' said Cicero. But in the end he did, saying he had died as the result of a shooting accident. His father had been a beater in a shooting party, and the Englishman could not handle a gun. He helped himself to more wine from the decanter, warming to his subject. Moyzisch tried not to interrupt, but occasionally prompted him to continue: 'Do you know the name of the Englishman who shot your father?'[6]

Cicero continued that he had received some compensation from the authorities, but it was not enough and he still hated the British. Cicero was telling Moyzisch what he thought he wanted to hear: 'I played on his credulity. What I said next burst out of me as if I were confiding to him as if it was a painful memory. The lie that I told him carried me away completely.'[7]

It was near 11 p.m before Cicero left, declining Moyzisch's offer of a lift. As he walked away into the night, he was '… filled with fear, fear of my father's anger. My father had died peacefully in his bed, and I had misused his memory.'[8]

Moyzisch returned to the embassy and locked the new films in the safe until morning; after his experience in Berlin, his enthusiasm for Operation Cicero was somewhat dented.

The next roll of film that was sent to Berlin caused some excitement there, much more than anything so far. It contained some handwritten notes about technical details. Moyzisch commented: 'I was told that it proved of immense value to the German Secret Service; they maintained that it helped them to break an important British cipher.'[9]

However, it was unlikely they could have been that valuable. Schellenberg saw the possibilities here and submitted copies of documents to *Chiffrierabteilung*, the cipher section of the High Command OKW, led by General Fritz Thiele. Documents also found their way to *Pers Z*, the Foreign Ministry deciphering office, either through Schellenberg or via the High Command. Some minor items were revealed in reusable codes, which Schellenberg labelled as a 'tremendous achievement.'[10] Moyzisch continued:

> The messages, which bore date-time notations, could help in breaking the British diplomatic codes, and though Pers Z would seem to be have been the logical recipient, Schellenberg gave the photographs to his communication-intelligence friends in the military. They cooperated fairly closely with Pers Z, however, and they probably passed the material to it. Pers Z may also have gotten copies from Ribbentrop. [Werner] Kunze and [Adolf] Paschke both saw Cicero documents and were unimpressed, for the British were by then superenciphering their most secret messages. They may have contributed to the solution of some lesser British systems and so helped produce some minor information, but they could not make possible the recovery of the one-time keys of any other messages.[11]

Of more importance was the detailed report on relations between Ankara and London. Much of it had been handwritten by the British ambassador, the main point being Turkey's determination to remain neutral. Von Papen called it: 'A lucid, sober draft, neatly arranged and elegantly formulated … Berlin won't enjoy this one very much.'

With the latest films, Moyzisch also sent a note stating that he had learnt a little about Cicero and the death of his father. He also pointed out that Cicero had destroyed one film of good material because he, Moyzisch, had been unavailable. He says he did this 'purely to annoy Ribbentrop'. However, he got a quick reply from the minister to instruct Cicero to take those photographs again. [12]

During this period, the bundles of notes under Cicero's carpet 'multiplied rapidly' and he enjoyed the feeling of walking on them. He had begun to mistrust Mara, and treated her with scorn. She complained of hardly seeing him, while he was concerned by her increasingly heavy drinking, which made her tongue loose, and her frequent and irritating questions:

> So far as I was concerned, she had outlived her usefulness. I had no more need to go to the house of Mr Busk, the First Secretary; everything I needed was within my reach in the Embassy. [13]

Over time, he increasingly felt his activities at the British Embassy were like a drug he could not resist. He photographed all he could find, doing the work with his new Leica camera in his servant's room. On one occasion he took documents from a black box by the ambassador's bedside, using his duplicate keys, while Sir Hughe, who had taken a sleeping pill, was asleep, before boldly putting them back without waking him. [14]

On another occasion he used Sir Hughe's telephone to contact Moyzisch and told him where he was, as if boasting. It was the only telephone in the embassy that was not connected to the switchboard. [15] This does appear overly risky. Yet Cicero not only had a degree of cunning, but quite a nerve to do what he did in the first place. No doubt he was high on adrenalin, which he seemed to enjoy.

Towards the end of November, Moyzisch considered going to Istanbul for Cicero, who had asked him to get £5,000 changed into US dollars. [16] Cicero could not change it at a local bank, for it would certainly attract attention, and he wanted the dollars for a business investment he had been offered. With the amount of documents he was supplying, Moyzisch felt it was a reasonable request.

However, later Moyzisch changed the money at 'our own bank in Ankara, where I asked the manager if he could change that much sterling into dollars'. Clearly he did this to avoid the long journey to

Istanbul, but he was lucky the bank had recently changed quite a large amount of sterling for dollars. Nevertheless, the bank manager later phoned Moyzisch after it had come to light the sterling he had changed for him was counterfeit. The money had ended up in England where it was declared no good, and it had been traced back to his bank in Ankara. Moyzisch signalled Berlin, who, denying any knowledge, instructed him to repay the bank out of embassy funds. Rumours began to emerge that larger denomination foreign banknotes were being printed in Germany for use in neutral countries.[17]

# 8

# ANDREAS TO BERNHARD

Having encountered counterfeiting rumours in Berlin, Moyzisch was suspicious of the reassurances he had been given. Surely, he thought, they would not 'be so foolish as to jeopardise the whole of Operation Cicero by paying him in bad notes?' Yet, he found he could not trust his masters at the SD. The amount of money was large and there appeared no limit on what they would pay; not once had they queried the scale of the payments. He took samples of the sterling banknotes from his safe, amounting to £10,000, which he took to a bank in Istanbul, well used by the German community. He told the manager they had been offered to the German Embassy for sale at a good rate and wanted to know if they were forgeries. He returned two days later to find the notes had been given the all clear. They were good.[1]

Maybe Moyzisch was lucky in choosing genuine notes, but this appears unlikely, or maybe the Istanbul bank was not up to spotting these accomplished copies. The fact was that the Germans did finance espionage with forged money, and Operation Cicero was not the first.

Most notably the two German agents, Johannes Eppler and Heinrich Sandstette, who were guided across the Sahara Desert by the explorer László Almásy, in an attempt to infiltrate British Headquarters in Cairo. Operation Kondor, which took place in May–July 1942 and was designed to aid Rommel's drive to the Nile, was funded by counterfeit money. Not only did the *Abwehr* send these agents out with forged money, but they were in far too large denominations, and also, as they should have been aware, British troops in Cairo were usually paid in Egyptian currency.[2] It was a 'colossal blunder of the most elementary kind' and led directly to their arrest.[3]

Another German agent, the double agent Eddie Chapman, was parachuted into England in December 1942 with £990 on him. The notes were contained in a moneybag and still had bands stamped with

'Reichsbank Berlin' and 'England' on them in pencil. Such a mistake would have led to the firing squad for a true German agent.[4]

Yet it was Bazna, in the guise of Cicero, who became the biggest dupe of Operation Bernhard – the German plan to use large amounts of counterfeit money to destabilise enemy economies, mainly the British. The early objective of the plan was not followed up, and it came to be used for critical purchases in other countries and to finance intelligence operations abroad.

The scheme had first been called Operation Andreas, with Alfred Naujocks the driving force behind the idea. At the beginning of the war he headed the SD document-forging section in Berlin. He was a rival of Schellenberg at that time and put his idea to Heydrich who, in turn, submitted it to Hitler, who approved the operation in November 1939. However, the British soon learnt of the scheme 'as a weapon of economic warfare' before the end of 1939.[5] They also shared this knowledge with the USA the following year, although Hitler had ruled out any copying of dollars at that time.[6] Yet the task before them was far greater than initially considered.

It was through Schellenberg's control of Bernhard that he was able easily to finance Cicero, though the huge amounts paid to Bazna were a mere drop in the ocean compared to what the scheme produced. Although Operation Andreas, during its eighteen months, produced only about £500,000 in fairly passable notes, but many technical difficulties were overcome in this period. With Naujock's fall from power – he was caught conducting illegal gold and currency transactions, and was behind sound recordings made of Heydrich while at the Berlin brothel, Salon Kitty – Andreas became largely inactive and its personnel dispersed. Heydrich had him relegated to the ranks and sent to the Eastern Front, where he served in the Waffen SS *Liebstandarte* 'Adolf Hitler' (bodyguard), which, by then, had grown to a divisional unit.[7] In 1943, due to ill health, he was sent to the west, where once more in favour and with Heydrich dead, he became economic administrator for the troops in Belgium, and was also involved in operations against the Belgian resistance.

In June 1941, Schellenberg took over the counterfeiting scheme when Heydrich made him head of Department VI SD-Overseas, although he had mixed views on taking over a failing section.[8] Andreas was left to wilt, with Schellenberg only occasionally sanctioning the use of notes already printed.

Heydrich was chief of the RSHA until 1942, but he was also appointed *Reichsprotektor* of Bohemia and Moravia in September 1941, a role that took up much of his time and energy. In the spring of 1942, an SOE team of Czech commandos, trained in Britain, parachuted into Czechoslovakia with orders to kill Heydrich. The assassination team, codenamed Anthropoid, had been in Prague some time when a heated meeting took place with local resistance leaders. A message was sent to London requesting the mission be called off, as it was likely to provoke harsh reprisals.

In London there was a delay, but the mission was not cancelled. According to Colonel Frantisek Moravets, the Czech head of military intelligence:

> I learned after the war that the British not only did not cancel the operation but continued to insist on it being carried out though without telling me.[9]

It was felt within the Czech resistance that Heydrich died because he was close on the trail of British agents and sympathisers within the German High Command. Admiral Canaris of the *Abwehr* is known to have had links to the SIS:

> [Stewart Menzies chief of the SIS (MI6)] knew Canaris's dilemma and he was, according to those who knew him well at this time, someone who would not shrink from ruthless, decisive action to help his opposite number as well as, more importantly, further his own services interests. 'Anthropoid' had not been an SIS mission but an SOE undertaking yet it is significant that at the moment of crisis over the future of the mission it was Menzies who Moravets sees on the British side and, if Moravets is to be believed, ensured that the mission was not called off.[10]

Whatever the reasons for Heydrich's death, it became the only assassination of a high-ranking German official in the war. He was attacked on 27 May in his car on the way to the office; he was struck by grenade fragments and died of his wounds on 4 June. However, as feared, a wave of terror was unleashed against the Czech population. The village of Lidice was destroyed on 9 June: 198 adult males were shot, all the women were deported to Ravensbruck concentration camp, and the children were taken to Germany for adoption.[11]

Following Heydrich's death, Himmler became chief of the RSHA, and day-to-day operations became the responsibility of Kaltenbrunner. In January 1943 he took over full leadership, and he had ordered Schellenberg to expand the counterfeiting operation in 1942. Hermann Dorner became head of section VI F 4, while Bernhard Kruger, an engineer, was appointed director of banknote production. So Operation Andreas became Operation Bernhard.[12]

Dorner and Kruger had their work cut out to get the operation running again. A special block, No. 19, was built at Sachsenhausen concentration camp, north of Berlin, and within a year they also had taken over block No. 18. The workforce was taken from political prisoners, mainly from concentration camps, with backgrounds in banking, printing and the paper industry. The printing machines came from the Ullstein works in Berlin; paper was delivered from the Hahmemuhle paper mill in Dassel; and inks came from Schmidt Bros and Kast und Ehringer in Berlin.[13]

Adolf Burger, who was one of the workers in the operation, says that work began:

> ... in September 1942, at first with a team of twenty-six prisoners. By December 1942 the machines and equipment were set up in Blocks 18 and 19, which were surrounded by barbed wire fencing. In January 1943 'Production B' started, i.e. the production of forged £5, £10, and £50 notes. August Petrick, a civilian wearing the gold Nazi Party badge supervised the prisoners, who were also guarded by sixteen secret service guardsmen.[14]

Once in full swing, the production operation proved efficient, and Kruger was concerned it would not be long before they reached the maximum total of currency that Himmler had set. He had no wish to be drafted to a military front, and his workers, the prisoners, feared for their lives should things come to an end; thus they conspired to slow the operation.[15]

Distribution of the growing amount of counterfeit notes created more problems. The original idea of 'bombing' Britain with banknotes was abandoned, said Schellenberg, 'because the air above Britain was too well defended, and our fuel situation was critical'.[16] However, he was reluctant to move large amounts of currency without the direct approval of Kaltenbrunner, which, in turn, meant going to Himmler and Hitler. The process was then geared towards the use of counterfeit money in SD operations; Hitler approved of the operation, with the proviso that the forged money was not used in occupied countries, although this restriction was often ignored. However, Schellenberg was not above using the forged money himself 'for the financing of enterprises abroad where I knew that I had to deal with cold-blooded and mercenary businessmen'.[17] Clearly, he felt Cicero would fall within this greedy group, for it was he that authorised payment in forged notes, a decision he was clearly happy with.[18]

Operation Bernhard continued long after Cicero disappeared from the scene. In September 1944, Kruger arrived at the forging plant to announce to his workers: 'Gentleman, from today we are going to produce dollars.'[19] This no doubt pleased the workers, as it ensured their lives would last that bit longer, though it was far too late in the war to have any effect.

By early 1945, Bernhard was no longer safe at Sachsenhausen and Himmler considered closing down the operation, but Kruger talked him into transferring the whole thing to Austria. Even with their house collapsing around them, petty rivalries between officials and departments continued, resulting in many delays. Finally they arrived at Mauthausen concentration camp, near Linz, in March 1945.

Adolf Burger viewed the new camp with horror:

> Mauthausen was like a fortress. The commander was SS-Standartenführer Franz Ziereis, a very brutal man, who had lampshades and other objects made out of the skin of tattooed victims.[20]

Kruger had not been with them in the move from Sachsenhausen to Mauthausen, and when he arrived he moved them to the smaller Redlzipf camp on 4 April 1945, so they had to pack up everything again. Burger continued:

> The SS men were raging, they cursed and swore and beat the prisoners they thought were not working fast enough. It was the first time they had behaved so brutally towards us in the special Kommando. The worse they treated us, the more we noticed that they feared for their lives, and that gave us some satisfaction.[21]

At Redlzipf the banknotes were stored underground in mine shafts that had been enlarged for production of the V1 flying bombs, and contained cranes and railway tracks. The forgery workshops were installed in two blocks. Production of dollar notes was due to start on 1 May, but orders soon arrived from Himmler to destroy everything, and all prisoners were to be returned to Mauthausen for liquidation. Kruger left those tasks to *SS-Untersturmführer* Hansch, while he made off with a large amount of good money obtained through his black market dealings. With the confusion all about them, and the US Army close by, much of the equipment and notes ended up in Alpine lakes, and many of the workers survived and were liberated.

Not all the counterfeit money went up in smoke or sank to the bottom of lakes, though. A truck load of sterling had been surrendered to Allied troops containing twenty boxes with a total of £21 million inside. Also much hurriedly abandoned currency was found floating in the Traun River by troops and civilians.

US Army Major George McNally, from Allied Headquarters in Frankfurt, and a British team investigated Operation Bernhard. They managed to trace about a third of the workers involved, as 133 of the 142 *Kommando* prison workers had been liberated by the Americans in Ebensee concentration camp on 6 May 1945.[22] Oskar Skala, one of three bookkeepers, was located in Czechoslovakia and still had his personal notebook.[23]

Sterling notes were produced in £5, £10, £20 and £50, to a total value of about £134 million. Only about £10 million were looked on as 'good' notes and, of that, £670,000 found their way to the RSHA. Only a small proportion of forged notes went abroad, mostly to Spain, Portugal and Switzerland, but £1.5 million went to Turkey and the Middle East.[24]

At the end of the war, Britain acted to protect its currency. From 1943 the only note bigger than £1 being issued was the white £5 note, and bigger denomination notes were removed relatively quickly. The magnitude of the discoveries in Austria and the scale of Operation Bernhard later forced the withdrawal of the £5 note as well. A new note was released in late 1945 with design differences from any copies that had been discovered.

# 9

# DECEMBER 1943

At the end of November 1943 the three Allied leaders, Churchill, Roosevelt, and Stalin, met in Tehran, their first meeting together. The two Western leaders assured Stalin that the invasion of France would definitely take place during the following year. Then Germany would be squeezed by Allied armies from the east, west and south.

It would not be long before Moyzisch would be looking at the minutes of the conferences at Cairo and Tehran, for December was to be Cicero's best period by far. He also observed Cicero seemed a changed man: he was more 'friendly', even 'talkative', and only if pressed on his background did he revert to type and clam up.[1]

Cicero and Sir Hughe Knatchbull-Hugessen had rapidly got used to each other. The valet had an enviable quality for a spy in that he merged into the background, as if becoming a mere comfortable fixture. He likened his life to watching a film he was not interested in: he woke the ambassador every morning at 7.30 a.m. with a glass of orange juice; he 'wished him good morning' and drew back the curtains; he 'pressed the ambassadorial trousers' and 'ran the ambassadorial bath'. Lady Knatchbull-Hugessen barely noticed him. They were as if 'all shadows passing without seeing each other.' Everything followed a familiar routine.[2]

Sir Hughe had been to Turkey many times before he took up residence as British ambassador in February 1939, only a few months before the great Mustafa Kemal Ataturk had died. Ankara was very much his monument. *The Times* published an obituary of the Turkish leader, dominated by pictures of the modern capital with new buildings, sports arenas and clinics.[3] The capital was a symbol of the new Turkey.[4]

By the time Cicero began work at the British Embassy, the staff had vastly increased: for Christmas dinner in 1939, Sir Hughe 'entertained the staff at a sit down dinner and we were nineteen'. By Christmas 1944 'we had two stand-up buffets of about one hundred and eighty each'.[5]

The embassy was extremely busy that winter of 1943–44, and Sir Hughe was preoccupied by efforts to try and bring Turkey into the war on the Allied side. He later wrote:

Whatever may be said on either side the truth is that it was at this moment that we entered upon the most difficult period in our relations.[6]

The mass of secret material increased, and with it the opportunities for Cicero, who was helped in this by Sir Hughe's frequent use of sleeping pills. One December night he entered the ambassador's bedroom, where the ambassador was in bed asleep, and spotted an empty glass of water on the bedside table by the black box: he '… had taken his sleeping pills as usual'. Silently using his duplicate keys, he opened the box and removed the papers. Once back in his room, he could not stop his hands from trembling.[7] Once composed he photographed the documents, noticing in Sir Hughe's handwriting the words: 'Papen knows more than is good for him'.

Returning the papers to the black box Cicero knocked over the tumbler, which smashed on the floor. The noise did not wake the ambassador and he merely moved in his sleep before lying still again. Cicero removed any broken glass and left.[8]

It's unclear whether the story is true. Even given Bazna's obvious attempt to embellish his actions, it does appear that Sir Hughe probably did take sleeping pills, or some sort of sedative. Sir Hughe later denied this when the story broke to the public in 1950. In a *Sunday Express* article, Knatchbull-Hugessen said he did not use sleeping tablets.[9] But he was under great strain and, with sleep difficult, it would have been understandable. Similarly, the amount of material Cicero was producing indicates easy access. Cicero also says he told Moyzisch the British ambassador took sleeping pills.[10]

What was certainly true was the reference to Von Papen knowing 'more than is good for him'. This was reported by Sir Hughe on 31 December to the security services. MI6 felt there was certainly a leakage somewhere and that it could be on 'the Turkish side'.[11] However, a short time later, direct from the US Office of Strategic Services (OSS), they were tipped off that a German agent had secured a British report on Turkish-British relations. 'C' compiled a report for Churchill that the 'information came from a good but not sure source'.[12] The OSS had an agent in the German Foreign Ministry, later identified as Fritz Kolbe.

December was not all plain sailing for Moyzisch, for orders came from Kaltenbrunner not to show Von Papen any Cicero documents. However, Moyzisch largely decided to ignore that directive. He even showed the ambassador the signal, who naturally fumed at his position being undermined and demanded Moyzisch show him 'all the material that passes through your hands'.[13] He had also been ordered to cut payment to Cicero to £10,000 per roll. Expecting trouble, Moyzisch broke the news once again using his friend's apartment, but Cicero was in a good mood. He helped himself freely to food and drink, confiding that once this was all over he would devote himself to music. He insisted on singing some arias for Moyzisch to demonstrate his good voice, and when the subject of money was broached, he readily agreed to the new scale of payment.

Moyzisch was also concerned about Cicero's appearance, for he had taken to wearing well-tailored suits of English cloth, and expensive handmade shoes. He told Cicero that his dress drew attention to him, and that people would wonder how a valet could afford such things. His behaviour was 'downright dangerous'. Cicero received the advice well and took off an expensive gold wristwatch he was wearing, asking Moyzisch to keep it for him until he could store it in Istanbul.[14]

From one meeting early in the month, which took place earlier in the day than usual, Moyzisch had to keep the films with him because he had to attend an official dinner. However, they began burning a hole in his pocket, so he and his wife got away as early as they could. Back at the embassy, he hurried off to the developing room and was stunned by their content. The films revealed the minutes of the Cairo and Tehran conferences.

He worked through the night and morning to produce a detailed report for Berlin. While typing this out at his secretary's typewriter, he felt the documents had shown him clearly 'what I was writing was nothing more nor less than a preview of Germany's destruction … Here a new world had been planned, whose premise was the utter blotting out of the Third Reich and the punishment of its guilty leaders.'[15]

That night he met Cicero again, and this new roll of film told him that the Turkish president, Ismet Inonu, had gone to Cairo with his foreign minister to meet with Roosevelt and Churchill. The Germans had had no idea that the Turkish president had even left Ankara.

By now, Cicero was meeting Moyzisch with new rolls of film every second or third day. On one of these meetings, while the Opel Admiral cruised 'the dark streets and alleys of Ankara' and Cicero sat smug in the back pleased with his work and reward, they picked up a tail. Moyzisch was temporarily blinded by headlights in his rear view mirror. There was a large dark limousine not far behind, and Moyzisch was glad he had gone to the trouble of obscuring his back licence plate with mud. He drove slowly waiting for the car to pass, but it kept station. He pulled into the curb to let it pass, but the following car did the same. Moyzisch moved off rapidly, speeding up trying to shake off the car behind. The Opel Admiral had a big six-cylinder engine of 3.6l, with a top speed of around 90mph.

Cicero seemed oblivious to what was happening and merely closed the curtains on the back window to reduce the glare. Moyzisch went faster, getting up to 75mph. The car behind sounded its horn. Again he slowed down, resorting to erratic changes of direction and speed.

Now Cicero had realised something was wrong. Moyzisch saw Cicero in the rear view mirror: 'He was hunched in his corner, deadly white.' Cicero resorted to chewing his fingernails, as he implored Moyzisch to go faster.[16] Moyzisch called Cicero a 'fool' for using the ambassador's telephone; it was surely British intelligence out there. They 'squabbled over whose fault it was,' says Cicero, but this would seem unlikely during a frantic car chase. Moyzisch says he tried an old trick: passing an intersection junction slowly, then swerving away at the last moment, accelerating hard around the corner, changing direction several times through a warren of streets where there was only inches to spare.

They emerged back onto Ataturk Boulevard, heading south, where he accelerated to 75mph and kept his 'foot pressed down, the accelerator flat against the floor-boards'. They raced past the German Embassy, before Moyzisch finally managed to shake off the pursuing car. Close to the British Embassy he slowed the car with 'screeching brakes' from 60mph to a crawl and let Cicero roll out. He returned to the German Embassy with no further trouble.

Cicero hoped the tail had been for Moyzisch and they, whoever they were, knew nothing about the man 'who had got in at Akay Street'. When he rolled from the car he kept low to the ground and found himself lying flat, his face near a garden fence, his body hidden in the dark shadows. He turned to see the Opel's taillights disappear, and then the other car speed past him. He saw only 'one occupant'. He thought he saw a face behind the wheel lit up by the dashboard lights: 'A young, smooth, expressionless face'.[17]

The car chase through the back streets of Ankara, Moyzisch felt, marked the first time 'somebody knew something about Operation Cicero who should not'. But who could it be? He did not think it was the British because nothing happened to Cicero, and he was more inclined to think it was the Turkish police or security services. But why would they follow him? Shortly after the car chase, while at a Jenkes' party, a Turkish Foreign Ministry official chided him that he should take more care driving 'particularly at night'.[18]

It later came to light that the likely occupant of the tailing car was an American intelligence agent, as Moyzisch was well known to other people in his line of work around the Turkish capital. It is also probable the Americans would have confided their observations to Turkish intelligence, for Turkey was 'a crucible of the secret war'.

It was conducted in Turkey's great twin cities of Istanbul and Ankara. It was the great stew of plots from all sides:

> ... as ambassadors and agents of every power, every cause and every faith intrigued beside the Golden Horn or down Boulevard Ataturk ... a host of nations jostled each other, spied upon each other, compromised each other, subverted each other, bribed each other, deceived each other in Serge's, the Phaia, the Station Restaurant, Papa Karpic's; and the boulevard came to be called 'The Rat Run'.[19]

The Cicero films of this period demonstrated to the Germans that Britain was pressing Turkey to enter the war, and had been doing so for some time. They had been aware of this, but they had far more details now and, more importantly, knew the stakes had been raised at four high-level meetings in 1943: at Moscow in October; at Cairo during Anglo-Turkish talks early in November; then at the main Tehran conference late in November; and another series of Anglo-Turkish talks in Cairo in December.

The Americans showed no interest in opening any new Balkan Front, for they had closely witnessed the last debacle, but it was still close to Churchill's heart, even after the Aegean fiasco, where British attempts to capture the Aegean Islands had been soundly defeated by what amounted to a scratch German force (see Chapter 10). Stalin encouraged the British, but he had little to lose, for it fell to them to handle the Turks.

# 10

# CHURCHILL'S FOLLY

From December 1942, Ambassador Sir Hughe Knatchbull-Hugessen and his team began putting pressure on the Turks, rather than trying to maintain the status quo as before. The war situation was much better for the Allies: 'With the Germans driven back, Libya and Cyrenaica clear, and Stalingrad relieved, the position was more favourable.'[1] Churchill suggested a meeting with the Turkish president and prime minister in Cyprus. However, the conference was held in Adana, the city lying 20 miles from the Mediterranean coast in south-central Anatolia.

Sir Hughe tried to cover his tracks by claiming he was going on a 'shooting expedition', setting out 'suitably attired in knickerbockers and with my guns ostentatiously placed in the car'. Then the party gathered at a small station in Kayash, east of Ankara. He wondered how successful the deception was as heavy snow had fallen, and along the road to Kayash were gangs of men clearing the way for the president's car. With Sir Hughe was A.K. Helm, his counsellor, and his aide Paul Falla. The Turkish President Ismet Inonu was accompanied by his Prime Minister M. Numan Menemencioglu and the Chief of the Turkish General Staff Marshal Fevzi Cakmak, with a host of advisors. Churchill came with his generals, Sir Harold Alexander, Sir Henry Maitland-Wilson, Sir Alan Brooke and several others in his entourage.

The conference was held on a disused railway loop, west of Adana, in the Turkish presidential train. The purpose of the meeting was outlined as 'an exploration of the likelihood and the desirability of Turkey taking an active part in the war during the year [1943]'.[2] However, Turkey was not prepared for war, but came to an understanding that the British might count on Turkey once 'they were adequately equipped'. Over the next few months, 'detailed conversations' would take place with military leaders and, as Sir Hughe commented: 'We were working toward a "Zero" hour timed for the autumn.'[3]

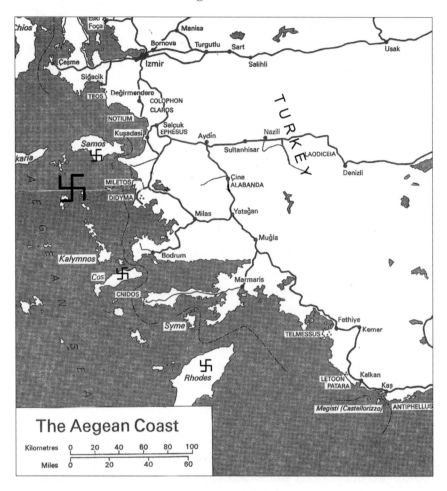

Aegean Coast 1943–44.

It was thought the meeting would have been kept secret, but the Turks soon released details of the conversations. It was also common knowledge that Churchill had received an enthusiastic welcome from the people of Adana. MI6 were well aware that Turkish ciphers might have sprung a 'leak' and the Turkish Foreign Ministry was in the habit of keeping other diplomatic missions 'informed of the progress of British/Turkish negotiations'.[4]

The British were surprised by the calm way the Germans viewed the Adana conference and the visit of British military leaders to Turkey. Von Papen believed he understood the Turkish position better than the British:

I had a perfect understanding with the Turkish statesmen; our friendship pact took second place to the Anglo-Turkish alliance, but the obligation in the latter to enter the war would only be fulfilled in extreme circumstances.[5]

By the autumn of 1943, those circumstances seemed to have arrived. In February 1943, General Sir Henry Maitland-Wilson had taken over as commander-in-chief, Middle East, and Churchill gave him four main tasks:

a) You will maintain the Eighth Army and support its operations to the utmost, until Tunisia is finally cleared of the enemy.
b) In conformity with the requirements of General Eisenhower, you will take all measures necessary for the mounting of that part of Operation 'Husky' which is launched from the area under your command.
c) You will make preparations for supporting Turkey in such measures as may be necessary to give effect to the policy of His Majesty's Government as communicated to you from time to time by the Chiefs of staff.
d) You will prepare for amphibious operations in the Eastern Mediterranean.[6]

Thus was born Operation Accolade to capture the Dodecanese Islands in the Aegean and induce Turkey to join the Allies. The Americans were not in favour and were convinced that 'Churchill's apparent obsession with the Eastern Mediterranean was influenced more than anything else by the prospect of post-war political gains'.[7] Conversely, the British chiefs of staff believed it important that Allied pressure should be maintained in the Mediterranean to aid the cross-Channel invasion of 1944.

The invasion of Sicily was followed by an invasion of the Italian mainland and Italy's surrender; on the Eastern Front the Russians were still advancing. Operation Accolade received US approval, but the British would have to go it alone when troops landed on Kos, Samos and Leros. The German reaction was swift and powerful, deploying over 300 aircraft to Crete. Air power would prove the key to the operation and, as only the British Bristol Beaufighter had the range to operate in that area, four squadrons of American long-range Lockheed P-38 Lightnings were requested.

Sir Hughe sent members of his own staff to the area, including his military attaché, Allan Arnold:

> A vital necessity was to ensure supplies of munitions and provisions for the forces which we had landed there. Without the slightest hesitation the Turkish Government came to our aid and supplies were shipped regularly from the Turkish mainland and communication facilitated with our forces in the Islands.[8]

The Germans were determined to deny the islands to the Allies and safeguard vital supplies of chrome ore, bauxite, aluminium and copper from Greece and Turkey. It was also important to keep the Romanian oilfields out of range of Allied heavy bombers. Thus German forces in the area did not hesitate on 8 September 1943 to implement Operation Axis and take over Italian positions when Italy surrendered.

German operations in the Aegean started with the islands of Karpathos, Siros, Andros, Tinos, Zea and Naxos. On 10 September, Lord Jellicoe, the commander of the Special Boat Service (SBS), parachuted into Rhodes in an attempt to get the Italian commander, Admiral Inigo Campioni, to hold the island for the British. At first the admiral was enthusiastic; however, as soon as he knew it would be several days before any substantial British forces could arrive on the island, his support disappeared. Two days later, the *Sturm-Division* took Rhodes and 40,000 Italian troops surrendered to the Germans. In spite of Rhodes now being hostile and across British lines of communication, Operation Accolade still went ahead as planned. Troops, including elements of the Long Range Desert Group, the Special Boat Service and several infantry battalions, were landed on Leros, Kos and Samos. Two Spitfire squadrons were established on Kos, although much more air support had to come from Cyprus, which was well beyond the range of single-seater fighters.

On 23 September the British destroyer *Eclipse* intercepted a German convoy with Italian prisoners from Rhodes and sank two transports and a torpedo boat. This led to the German invasion of Kos and Leros to eliminate them as British air and naval bases. *Luftwaffe* strength had now increased to 400 aircraft operating from Rhodes and Crete. Subsequent air attacks sank the Royal Navy destroyers *Queen*, *Olga* and *Intrepid* in Portolago harbour, Leros, and they pounded Kos airfield, making it inoperable.

On 1 October, the Royal Navy in Alexandria dispatched all available fleet destroyers to escort the battleships *Howe* and *King George V* to Malta. This left only 'Hunt'-class destroyers in the Aegean, despite the knowledge that the German invasion of Kos was imminent – an odd decision. Destroyers and other warships were dispatched to the Levant when they became available, while six Lightning squadrons of the US Twelfth Air Force were deployed to Gambut, Libya, to support the Royal Navy.[9]

General Dwight D. Eisenhower, Allied Supreme Commander, was far from happy with this:

> If the decision to undertake Accolade depends upon a firm commitment for the diversion from our own operations of a material portion of our air force, then Accolade will have to be postponed. We will be inferior to the enemy in ground strength throughout the winter. Our air force is the asset that we count on to permit us taking the offensive in spite of this fact. Our first purpose must remain.[10]

Churchill appealed directly to President Roosevelt the next day:

> I believe it will be found the Italian and Balkan peninsulas are militarily and politically united and that really it is one theatre with which we have to deal ...
>
> I beg you to consider this and not let it be brushed aside and all these possibilities lost to us in the critical months that lie ahead.[11]

However, it was all too late. Kos was invaded on 3 October and, by the next day, the garrison had surrendered, with over 1,300 being taken prisoner and 102 Italian officers who had co-operated with the British executed, including the commanding officer, under Hitler's 11 September order to execute captured Italian officers.

The invasion of Leros was delayed when a troop convoy was surprised by the Royal Navy and a transport was sunk with heavy loss of life. The US Lightnings were also effective, shooting down dozens of German aircraft. But the cost to the Royal Navy was heavy: four destroyers were sunk and the anti-aircraft cruiser *Carlisle* was damaged and towed to Alexandria, never to put to sea again. Just when the Lightnings were having a marked effect, however, they were recalled to the central

Mediterranean, and the British never recovered from the withdrawal of these outstanding aircraft.

By the time the invasion of Leros began on 12 November, the Germans had complete control of the air. The fighting on the island was vicious; the Germans largely arrived by sea and air during the day, and the British reinforced and re-supplied the garrison at night. Royal Navy destroyers also bombarded German positions on the island, while motor torpedo boats conducted sweeps in the hope of catching German forces at sea.

Slowly, after much hard fighting on the island, the German paratroops and Brandenburg Regiment gained the upper hand. The British commanding officer, Brigadier Robert Tilney, decided on 16 November to surrender the island. The LRDG and the SBS refused to surrender and escaped from the island. About 3,200 British and 5,350 Italians were taken prisoner. Tilney did manage to save most of the Italians from the threatened massacre by the Germans that had occurred on other islands, most notably Cephalonia.

Cicero had only just come on the scene to witness the reaction within the embassy to the first British defeat since Tobruk in June 1942. Sir Hughe felt:

> At this particular moment the progress of the war on the widest lines was all towards Allied victory, but the lesson of German air power in the Dodecanese could not safely be disregarded.
>
> It was also pretty clear to the Allies that at the moment Turkey should not be pressed into an active part in the war or confronted with any major proposals during 1943.[12]

However, Churchill's view was that the Turks should be brought off the fence and out of the comfort of neutrality; the defeat in the Dodecanese was only a delay. He ordered his representatives to concentrate their efforts to get Turkey into the Allied fold.

Therefore, it would fall to Sir Hughe, or 'Snatch' as he was known within the Foreign Office, to lead the assault on German power in Turkey. As a result, he was often fully briefed on most major British and Allied decisions, and herein lay the opportunity and danger of espionage.[13]

# 11

# THE TURKISH LABYRINTH

In the autumn and winter of 1943, a series of conferences were held to take stock of the general war position on the Allied side, the first taking place in Moscow in October. In November, Anthony Eden, on his return from Moscow, met the Turkish Foreign Minister, M. Numan Menemencioglu, in Cairo, where the case for Turkey's early entry into the war was put during three days. The British pushed for a minimum of the free use of Turkish air bases.

The Turks wanted to know what was expected of their army, and they did not want to merely become an Allied air base. For the Turks, the British proposition felt like entering the war at the 'eleventh hour and was clearly distasteful', like the 'unheroic role which Mussolini had played'. Yet, on the other hand, they were uneasy about the German power that had been clearly demonstrated on their border in the Dodecanese. Also there was Stalin to be considered; the Turks, as ever, never trusted the Russians.

It was decided the Turkish party would return home and report to the government in Ankara. There, after a long debate, Sir Hughe was informed Turkey would enter the war. But, and there was always a 'but' in dealings with the Turks, this could only take place if Turkey was adequately defended. Given the amount of supplies already provided, Sir Hughe felt 'the Turkish view lacked justification'.[1]

The Turkish president was invited to attend the next Cairo conference, scheduled for December following the Tehran meeting, where he would meet with Roosevelt and Churchill. Sir Hughe conveyed the invitation; he recalled a similar invitation the previous year for a meeting in Cyprus, before he had been informed: 'it was unconstitutional for the President to leave the country'. So he felt there was little prospect of the Turkish president attending. Yet the reply in this case was positive, and was a clear 'indication of their attitude'.

If the president was being asked to the Cairo conference just to hear the decisions made in Tehran, then he would not go. But if the meeting was 'an opportunity for free and unprejudged discussions' as to Turkey's role in 'the common cause, the president would accept'. The assurances requested in this case were given.[2]

The president's party left on 3 December and the delegates in Cairo were housed in luxury 'and most hospitably provided with everything they could require, from sherry and cigars downward'.[3] Not that their arrival was unexpected, for on 14 November the *Egyptian Gazette* ran a story that Mena House, a former royal residence, was to be used for important talks. Chester Morrison of the *Chicago Sun* newspaper said: 'Everything about this whole business was very secret except that nearly everybody knew about it.'[4]

Even the leaders took in the sights, with Churchill taking Roosevelt to see the Pyramids of Giza, with the obligatory Egyptian dragoman and a large escort. The next day the dragoman sold his story to several papers, making more money out of an afternoon's work than he did in a year. Major A. W. Sansom of Field Security in Cairo was glad to see the back of them: 'Finally they all flew off, the enclave was dismantled, and Cairo returned to normal.'[5] So much was going on that the British felt, and hoped, the Germans would be confused; after all, they had broadcast late in November that Roosevelt, Churchill and Stalin had met there 'in a tent' beside the Pyramids. What the Germans broadcast and what they knew a few days later, thanks to Cicero, was very different.[6]

The Turks remained convinced throughout that the nation's real role would be to provide air and naval bases, and this would expose them to land and air attack. Sir Hughe admitted:

> It is impossible to deny that there was ground for these suspicions.
>
> Unless I am mistaken the Tehran decision as to Turkey's early entry into the war was never formally communicated to the Turks.[7]

Yet, in private, the Turks did not feel threatened by an invasion along their Balkan border, given the ebbing strength of the Axis powers.

Britain had already been engaged in training Turkish Air Force pilots and improving their airfields, with Operation Saturn basing RAF squadrons and radar at these bases. Initially, forty-nine squadrons were envisaged, but with Operation Overlord barely six months away, even

Churchill concluded this commitment had to be reduced to no more than twenty.

The Turks felt the amount was inadequate to cover western Anatolia and vital parts of the country.[8] This was primarily a result of their experience in the First World War, in which, they believed, they had been tricked into the war by Germany. Turkish interests had barely been considered during the conflict. Thus the Cairo talks ground toward stalemate.

The issue of British technicians within Turkey, mainly RAF personnel, was another area of dispute. Britain wanted 2,000 men described as 'infiltrators'; Turkey felt this was far too many, close to a declaration of war, and that these people were looked on with suspicion in the country. Thus Ankara insisted on no more than 250. A long meeting took place on 18 December between Sir Hughe and Menemencioglu, and the British ambassador believed he had negotiated an increase in the number of people, but it soon became clear Turkey would question the need 'for every single technician'.[9]

The Turkish government also flatly refused the request for a visit by Britain's three regional service chiefs. Sir Hughe wrote: 'Whatever may have been at the back of the Turkish mind, it was on these obstacles that hopes of immediate agreement broke down'.

At last the conference ended with the arrangement that: 'the Turkish Government should state their attitude by February 15th, 1944, the immediate point for decision being whether they would allow the use by us of their air bases'.[10] Churchill was reluctant to allow his Balkan strategy to fail, so he kept his officials badgering the Ankara government.

The British military mission, led by Air Marshal Sir John Linnell, spent most of January 1944 trying to find a way through the 'Turkish Labyrinth', but at last gave up and withdrew. These talks were deliberately prolonged to mislead the Germans. Much material earmarked for Turkey was diverted to air bases in Italy, where it could be put to better use. However, thanks to Cicero, the Germans were already aware of the failure of British plans.[11] Von Papen wrote:

> We obtained indisputable evidence of Turkey's attitude to increasing Allied pressure. We also learnt that the possibility of an Allied attack on the Balkans through Salonica could be ruled out. This was of great importance, because it meant there was no need for the considerable dispersal of our defensive forces which the indifferent communications

in this region would otherwise have made necessary. The Supreme Command now realized that the only real threat with which it had to contend was the invasion of France ...[12]

It does appear that, at the least, Menemencioglu was playing off both sides in a misguided attempt to extend Turkish borders at Bulgarian expense. However, Britain took this stand to be pro-German and began to cool relations. Sir Hughe, often supportive of the Turks, acknowledged that 'we made no attempt to conceal our disappointment' from the Turks.[13]

Menemencioglu was at the centre of another crisis at the end of December, which indirectly got Moyzisch into hot water. Alerted by the Cicero documents, Von Papen felt he had no choice but to protest directly to Menemencioglu over the British construction of radio aircraft guidance stations and more British technicians arriving in the country. Von Papen tried to cover his source by saying he 'had heard the British air attaché or one of his colleagues had mentioned such plans to certain neutrals'.[14] He drew attention to likely German reprisals that could include the bombing of Istanbul.

The minister said he felt Von Papen was misinformed. The same day, Menemencioglu informed Sir Hughe what had been said and alerted him to a possible leak. As we now know, Sir Hughe in turn alerted the British Foreign Office that Von Papen knew much more 'than was good for him'.[15]

Moyzisch was reading this signal less than thirty hours later, after developing the film, and he 'had no illusions about the probable consequences' once Berlin realised he had disobeyed orders about showing documents to the ambassador. Moyzisch considered not sending in the roll of film covering these events, but then he would have to replace the £10,000 paid for it. He even thought about trying to raise the money himself to cover this, but knew he would have difficulty obtaining that amount of sterling. He had no choice but to send in the documents and films: he 'sealed the documents in the usual envelope. I felt as though I were posting off my own death-warrant.'[16]

Yet, in effect, little happened, though Moyzisch was unnerved by 'Kaltenbrunner's icy silence'. A week later, a letter arrived from the SD leader, marked 'To Be Opened Personally'. The letter informed him that he would be held 'responsible for a gross breach of discipline in disobeying strict orders' — essentially, a written warning. Ribbentrop had nothing to say about the situation, which clearly annoyed Moyzisch.[17]

Von Papen was left largely on his own with the information: 'At no time did I receive from either Hitler or Ribbentrop any instructions ...' This was a situation he found bizarre in the extreme: 'Any other Foreign Minister would tell an ambassador forwarding such priceless information what they thought of it and what steps they expected him to take.'[18]

Moyzisch concluded that Cicero was in danger, as the British had been made aware of the leak, although 'these suspicions did not seem to point in any particular, let alone the right direction'. There was another cause for concern that Moyzisch was unaware of — Cicero's tangled love life.[19]

# 12

# A TRANSFER OF AFFECTIONS

As the stack of banknotes under Cicero's carpet began to grow in his little room at the British Embassy, his character began to change, and not for the better: his dress and appearance changed, as did his sexual relationship with the slender, blue-eyed, black-haired Mara. He began to treat her with 'contempt', and her complaints at not seeing him were brushed aside: 'So far as I was concerned, she had outlived her usefulness'.[1]

Yet she was a potential danger to him, as she had a direct link to the First Secretary at the British Embassy, being the nanny to Douglas Busk's child. Bazna began to suspect Mara might betray him, and pondered whether she would take 'vengeance' on him.[2] Instead, he seemed to court further danger, by taking up with a new mistress, Esra, who was barely 17. He says she was the daughter of a distant cousin, Mehmet, who wanted Bazna to find a good post for her in Ankara; after all, she was 'well educated' and had attended a 'commercial college'. He informed Mara they would have to make room for her.[3]

Mara flew into a rage at the mere suggestion, saying she did not want her in 'their house'. Bazna replied that he was duty bound through family ties to help the girl.

'Esra will not come and live here,' said Mara. 'You're working for the Germans. Now I know and that's why she won't come and live here.'

Bazna says, at that point, he 'smacked her face hard'.[4]

He was surely playing with fire and, although we only have his word for it, it is clear he enjoyed living on the edge. British intelligence would later call Bazna's account 'worthless as evidence'.[5] However, we do know Mara worked for the Busks, as Bazna did for a while, and it is also clear she did not betray him.

She even alerted him, surprising him by her fidelity, that she had overheard Mr and Mrs Busk talking about the Germans having a good source of secret information, maybe in the ambassador's residence. Bazna was unsure whether to believe her, but when he went to the embassy he was on guard, suspecting any stranger he met was a spy watching him.

With the imminent arrival of Esra, Bazna tried to get her a job at the embassy as a maid. His approach to Lady Knatchbull-Hugessen failed, but she did say his niece, as Bazna described her, could stay at the embassy until she found accommodation elsewhere. He was pleased with himself, feeling that if he had been under suspicion she would have rejected his request 'out of hand'. Also for the moment, it solved the problem of Esra staying at his villa and the likely clash with Mara.

On the same day, he says, while Sir Hughe was playing the piano, he could not resist bursting into song, singing from the 'Flying Dutchman'. The ambassador was highly amused by this and got into a brief discussion on music. Bazna confided to him that he had 'attended the conservatoire in Istanbul'. It must have been a busy day as, while photographing more documents, he learnt about a planned Allied air raid on Sofia.[6]

Not long after this, Mara told him she had heard Mr Busk tell his wife that security men had arrived from London. They were led by the senior Foreign Office official Sir John Dashwood, who arrived in Ankara at the end of January.[7]

Bazna quickly removed all the incriminating things from his room – money, films and photographic equipment – in case there was a search of servant's quarters; he hid them under the stairs, so no suspicion would fall on him if they were found.

Mara and Bazna had another row when he told her Esra had arrived; he says she was 'overwhelmed' by 'fear and jealousy'.[8] However, Mrs Busk was about to return to Britain with the baby and wanted Mara to go with them. Bazna encouraged her to go. He even claims that Mara bade him a tearful farewell when leaving for Britain, and Esra then became his mistress.

He found Esra bewitching: he was twenty years older than her; she was 'fair, like many Turks of Greek origin'; and she had a captivating effect on the other male servants at the embassy, which probably increased Bazna's lust for her. He told her she dressed 'badly' and was 'too loud', and he doubted he could obtain a position for her at the embassy.[9] Like Mara, he bought Esra expensive clothes and had her hair done. Only four days after she arrived, he says he confided to her that he was a spy. It made him more colourful, he wanted her to become his 'audience', just as Mara had been. 'I felt like a hero in a spy play; Esra was an admiring spectator in the box who would afterwards ask for my autograph.'[10]

Unlike Mara, Esra became directly involved in his work as a spy and, during her brief time at the embassy, she helped him find out how to deactivate a new electrical alarm used on Sir Hughe's study safe. But her presence did not last long. Lady Knatchbull-Hugessen asked about Esra, and Bazna again sought a position for her. However, 'Madam' was cold in her reply, reminding him that Esra's stay was only temporary. Bazna wondered if he might have gone too far and Esra was sent to the rented villa.

In Berlin, there were still doubts in some quarters about the Cicero material. These had been heightened in mid-December by one photographed document, on which appeared two fingers holding the papers while the picture was taken. Moyzisch knew it was Cicero because he identified the signet ring on the index finger.

Moyzisch's first reaction was that: '[If the] British should ever get hold of this print it would mean the end for Cicero'.[11] But, he wondered, how else could Cicero hold the documents and take the photograph? He knew this would cause 'consternation in Berlin'.

As soon as the documents arrived, Moyzisch was bombarded with questions, which drove him 'frantic'. Berlin sent a photographic expert to Ankara. Moyzisch's office was bugged with hidden microphones and Cicero was persuaded to come there. He was praised on his skill with a camera; the flattery worked and Cicero explained his working technique. The expert concluded it was unlikely, but not impossible, that Cicero worked alone. The expert returned to Berlin and, although Moyzisch 'never saw the official report', he was 'no longer pestered by telegrams which I was quite unable to answer'.[12]

Schellenberg was satisfied, as he felt 'from the beginning' that Cicero did not work alone. But this did not overly matter or cast doubt on the material as far as he was concerned.[13] However, the Sofia documents, outlining the Allied bombing offensive for the German satellite states in 1944, finally satisfied most of the doubters. The Bulgarian capital was attacked by Allied aircraft on 10 January, flying from air bases in southern Italy. During the day, 143 American B-17 Flying Fortresses bombarded the city, while forty-four British Wellingtons attacked at night, with over 1,500 people killed or wounded and 400 buildings destroyed. Subsequent raids on Sofia killed or injured 3,000 people and destroyed

2,600 buildings, while the Allies lost 117 aircraft.[14] Sofia lacked any real air defences, so air raids caused considerable terror to the population.[15] In addition, Captain Gerhard Wengel, *Luftwaffe* commander of I/JG 5 Fighter Wing, was killed when his aircraft was shot down by an American Lightning during the raid.

Moyzisch was surprised by Berlin's callous attitude in not warning the Bulgarian authorities, just to prove that the Cicero documents were genuine. Afterwards he 'wondered if Berlin was satisfied' with the thousands of casualties.[16] Schellenberg says that Sofia was 'forewarned in ample time, though there was nothing much that could be done to counter the attack'.[17] If this was done, it is likely that only military units were alerted.

Von Papen says he was surprised when later reading about the Sofia raid in Moyzisch's book, because these were documents he had not been sent. After Kaltenbrunner's warning, Moyzisch was more inclined to obey SD orders.[18]

In one of the Sofia air raid shelters that day, terrified by the raid, was Cornelia Kapp, a secretary working at the German Embassy in the city. Known to Moyzisch as 'Elisabet', she was another young woman who would play a vital role in the Cicero story.[19]

# 13

# TO CATCH A SPY

According to the British files, they were first alerted to a possible security problem in Ankara towards the end of December 1943. The US State Department reported that an agent at the Hungarian Legation in Stockholm revealed a leakage from the Cairo talks and that the Germans 'appeared to have full details of the conference'.[1]

The British in Ankara first believed it was more likely a Turkish problem. However, Sir Hughe Knatchbull-Hugessen himself reported on 31 December that the German ambassador, Von Papen, knew too much. The British economic warfare agent in Turkey at the time, John Lomax, was informed by one of his Turkish agents, who worked close to the Turkish president Ismet Inonu, that there was a spy at the British Embassy. But this came later, towards the end of January 1944.[2]

It was Fritz Kolbe, who worked at the German Foreign Ministry while in Bern, Switzerland, in August 1943, who offered important ministry documents to the British. But the British military attaché, Colonel H.A. Cartwright, turned him away – a bad blunder. Kolbe was not to be so easily dissuaded, however, and turned to the Americans. Allen Dulles was the OSS man in Bern and he snapped up the offer. Kolbe's work at the Foreign Ministry included screening cable traffic for OKW, the military high command. Codenamed 'George Wood', Kolbe was strongly opposed to the Nazis and was willing to supply anything he felt important to the Allies in a bid to hasten the end of the war. He supplied another batch of material in October and kept in touch with Dulles for over a year, with the American often sharing material with the British.

Another batch came from Kolbe in December and contained some of Cicero's work. In January, Dulles gave these documents to an MI6 agent in Bern, Fredrick Vanden Heuvel, known as 'Fanny'.[3] Dulles says that, a few days after this, Heuvel came to see him, asking him to forget Cicero as London was 'aware' of the case. Dulles thought that 'the British were playing some sort of game with Cicero'.[4]

Heuvel was a papal count and director of Eno's Fruit Salts. He had been recruited for MI6 by Colonel Claude Dansey, who would become assistant chief of the wartime SIS, and in his career he worked for both MI5 and MI6. He was a bellicose man and colleagues found 'there was nothing he'd enjoy more than having a scrap'. He hated intellectuals and felt 'every man had his price and every woman was seducible'.[5] Heuvel's actions were on the orders of Dansey, who disliked Dulles and dismissed the Kolbe material as a plant – a mistake that marked the end of his career.[6] He passed the material to Felix Henry Cogwell to prove his theory; it is clear he did little with the documents, but passed them to a junior at SIS.

That junior was later to be the notorious Soviet spy, Kim Philby, who studied the documents on their 'merits'. He did a rather obvious thing and had them checked by cryptographic experts to see 'whether they had already received intercepted messages matching the Dulles material'. The majority were telegrams received by the German Foreign Office from missions abroad. He then sent a series of messages from the German military attaché in Tokyo to OKW through diplomatic channels.

Two days later, Commander Alexander ('Alistair') Denniston, head of the Government Code and Cypher School (GC & CS) at Bletchley Park, contacted Philby in 'a state of some excitement' with news that three telegrams matched already deciphered telegrams. The others would help in breaking the German diplomatic code, and could he have more.

Philby circulated the documents to other departments as genuine. Dansey soon got wind of this and a cold interview took place with Philby, in which he still tried to dismiss the OSS findings.

Philby found this strange, after all, 'Not even our own circulating sections, let alone departments, knew that OSS was involved. They regarded it as our stuff, they were asking for more. It seemed that the credit was ours.' This appeared to be Dansey's biggest concern, so he finally conceded the point. It was then left to Philby to handle any more material:

To my surprise, the case was by no means closed. Our German friend [Kolbe] proved to be an intrepid operator, and paid several more visits to Bern with his useful suitcase.[7]

The much heralded exploits of Station X, Bletchley Park, through the 'Ultra' decrypts, a carefully guarded secret during the Second World War and for many years after, had no direct effect on Cicero. No intercepted signals revealed the source, only that a breach in security at Ankara had occurred. Cicero operated for a relatively short period and so, given the wealth of information arriving at Bletchley Park, it was probably given a low priority and the bird would have long flown before much was revealed. 'Ultra' referred to the breaking of the German Enigma machine cipher. From June 1941 the term 'Ultra Secret' was used; this is said to have been the idea of Commander Geoffrey Colpays and taken from the fact that the codebreaking success was considered more important than the highest security classification at the time, 'Most Secret'.[8]

General William Donovan, head of the OSS, had passed the Dulles report to President Roosevelt, who, in turn, informed Churchill about the likely leak in Ankara, and that the Germans had details on the Cairo Conference and, in particular, the 6 December minutes on 'Operation Saturn'. Churchill replied in a telegram drafted for him by 'C', Sir Stewart Menzies:

> Thank you for drawing my attention to this matter. I am assured that our respective Intelligence Services are closely collaborating on this subject and an investigation has been ordered.[9]

Despite Churchill's wishes, the various security services did not work together well on Cicero, or often on matters other than at the highest level under the Joint Intelligence Committee (JIC), formed in 1936. Although the JIC did not get off to a good start, badly misjudging the Nazi-Soviet Pact and the Polish crisis at the outbreak of war, it was better during the war, though often slow to grasp the significance of intelligence.[10]

Below the JIC were MI5, the Security Service responsible for counter-espionage at home, and MI6, the Secret Intelligence Service, in charge of espionage abroad. MI5 worked closely with the Home Office, MI6 with the Foreign Office, and both with various military branches. The Special Operations Executive, however, came under the Ministry of Economic Warfare.

Section V of MI6 was responsible for the security of embassies, while SIS attachés working from these buildings often conducted field operations. Lieutenant Colonel Montague (Monty) Chidson was the assistant military attaché in Ankara and the MI6 man in the area. He tried to tighten security, but often fell foul of Sir Hughe and, by the time of the leaks, they were barely on speaking terms. He was far from being a top drawer SIS operative, with one account labelling him as a 'disastrous' station agent.[11]

The friction between Chidson and the ambassador was over document security. Working practices were improved and a search conducted for listening devices, though Sir Hughe still felt the Turks were the more likely source. However, once the Kolbe papers had revealed Cicero, the Foreign Office informed him of the discovery, and that they were sending out two experts to investigate.

'Genial' and 'jovial' Sir John Dashwood, Foreign Office security officer, and Chief Inspector Cochrane of Special Branch duly arrived.[12] They tried to find out how the Germans got hold of the papers, and their second task was to further tighten security.

Sir Hughe was not pleased with the arrival of the team and Dashwood had to proceed 'with considerable tact' in dealing with the ambassador.[13] Using the enemy telegrams, they tried to find out where the corresponding papers had been when copied, and thus who might have access to them. Here Sir Hughe may have led them astray with his conviction that the leak had most likely taken place on a train 'either on the way to or from Cairo', as the German documents 'corresponded closely to the briefs he had carried in a brown travelling box' when he had gone to Adana in December. He had left the box 'unattended, in his carriage while he was in the restaurant car'.[14]

It was noted rather 'wearily' in the security files: 'We must recognise that His Excellency does not habitually differentiate between convenience and security'.[15] Sir Hughe went on to point the finger of suspicion at one of Inonu's staff who had left the restaurant car early; it was surely he who had photographed the documents.

Dashwood was not convinced by this, but there was no way to prove or disprove it. He and Cochrane questioned all the embassy servants and searched all their rooms. Beforehand, Cicero had moved everything that might incriminate him, while the money had been taken to the villa and locked in a desk.

Sir Hughe called Bazna to his room for the interview on the pretext that they required coffee. In the room Bazna found three other men with the ambassador who were intent on examining the safe. Bazna felt they were all scrutinising him, before Sir Hughe asked him how long he had been his valet.

'Three months, Your Excellency,' he answered in French.

Sir Hughe said he was satisfied with him. Bazna says they tried him with English, which he answered, then German, asking for sugar, to which he replied, 'I hardly understand German'.

The ambassador intervened in French that they required milk and sugar. Bazna commented that Sir Hughe '… seemed to disapprove of these secret service methods; he had too much delicacy of feeling for this world'.[16]

It appears they dismissed Bazna as a suspect because 'the valet was too stupid to make a good spy and did not, in any case, speak or understand English'.[17]

However, why was Sir Hughe not more suspicious of Bazna? The leaks had started roughly when he arrived, although he had been in the Busks' service before. In 1930, Knatchbull–Hugessen had been appointed minister to the three Baltic States with his legation at Riga. In this decade, the countries became coveted as a buffer zone by both Germany and Russia, and, with the rise of Hitler, 'Sections of them became sympathetic to Nazi ideals, especially in Estonia where certain groups were active enough to cause anxiety'.[18]

It was against this background that the ambassador's new valet, who had outstanding references but questionable habits, became an agent of the *Abwehr*. The valet, called Tony, had been a prostitute to wealthy homosexuals and was no doubt blackmailed into becoming a spy. Again a duplicate key was used to copy documents from dispatch boxes.

However, Tony's antics with boyfriends in the residence attracted the attention of the SIS man at the legation, Captain Arthur Leslie Nicholson, a career intelligence man, who alerted the ambassador. Tony was warned but not sacked, and remained there until 1940.[19]

Had Sir Hughe forgotten Tony? Or did he not take Captain Nicholson's warnings seriously? Or did he think it could not happen twice? The affair was reported to higher authority, but it appears no one knew about the copied documents, and the Germans were only just being looked on as a serious threat.

Dashwood returned to London far from satisfied with the investigation. Later he wrote a report on the matter, laying much of the blame for the leaks at Sir Hughe's door: '... having cleared all other elements of the British staff'.[20] By the time he did conclude that Bazna was Cicero, the valet had resigned and disappeared. A story did circulate that Dashwood almost caught Cicero in the act by sitting in Sir Hughe's study in the dark. Yet even if this did happen, there would be all sorts of reasons a valet would enter the room, so it is really fanciful and surmised with the benefit of hindsight.[21]

Given that Bazna continued his work after the investigation finished, he must have somehow by-passed the electrical device on the safe. He says it was he, with Esra's help, who identified which fuse in the fuse box controlled the safe lock. Bazna argued with the electrician doing the work that he needed to press Sir Hughe's suits, but there was no power for the iron, and the ambassador would be angry if they were not ready.[22] Esra had removed the fuses at the workmen's request and, while she watched, they replaced all the others except the safe fuse.

Cicero confided to Moyzisch that an investigation was being conducted at the British Embassy, and told him about the updates to the safe and a 'lucky chance that enabled him to find out how to open the safe once more'.[23] He had listened in on conversations about the safe's new mechanism, but he did not mention Esra's part in the discovery.

Moyzisch picked up on this, for Cicero had told him before that he could not speak English, although the SD man had never really believed that. He withheld this information from Berlin for it would have 'meant more trouble for me'. He felt this was just a ploy by the artful Cicero to increase the price and, sure enough, a few days later, he insisted the work was much more dangerous and wanted £20,000 per roll of film. Moyzisch refused.

The quality of the material was also not as good as it had been. A roll of film developed after the investigation contained a 'statement of accounts of petty expenditure'. Moyzisch felt the British ambassador would not keep such papers in the safe and Cicero was just after easy pickings. He told him he could not pay 'for that sort of rubbish'. However, he sent the roll of film with a covering letter to Berlin, and was surprised by the reply: 'I was curtly told to pay Cicero his £10,000 and informed that this roll had proved extremely valuable'.[24]

About this time in January, Bazna took Esra to the ABC department store on Ataturk Boulevard and bought her a 'beautiful, soft, fur lined coat'. Snow was on the ground and the 'Siberian winter that prevails in

Anatolia was at its height'. He questioned her as they walked along, the snow crunching beneath their feet. Could she remember which fuse it was that controlled the safe?

She said she was 'not sure'.

Bazna replied, in that case, 'I have to make up my mind whether I can use you or not.'[25]

By now the war had turned decisively against Germany. In December, the last big German warship, the battle cruiser *Scharnhorst*, was sunk in the Battle of the North Cape by a British fleet. While in January, the Russians broke the two-year German siege of Stalingrad, and the RAF launched its biggest raid on Berlin, with 600 bombers dropping 2,300 tons of bombs on the city.

It was about this time that Cicero says he began to see increased references to 'Overlord' in the documents he photographed.[26] The Germans were aware of the codename by November 1943, and it may well have been the Cicero documents that alerted them.[27]

# 14

# DEFECTIONS

Having to deal with Cicero had increased Moyzisch's workload hugely, with much of it during unsociable hours. And when his secretary, 'Schnurchen', caught her thumb in the office safe in September, she was reduced to typing with one hand and he was on the lookout for extra help. 'Schnurchen' was a nickname meaning 'Clockwork' or everything under control. She was to him, 'Efficient, tidy, reliable and loyal', a 'rare phenomenon, the perfect secretary'.[1]

He was reluctant to apply to the powers in Berlin for help. However, during December the press attaché, Seiler, had gone to Sofia on official business and, in an air raid shelter, he met 'Elisabet' and her parents.

For reasons best known to Moyzisch, he insisted on giving this young woman a pseudonym in his account, saying: 'For the sake of the girl's family I do not propose to reveal her real identity.'[2] More likely, it was to conceal his mistakes in the Cicero case and in hiring her. Von Papen does not name her either, but says she was an 'employee of the Gestapo'.[3] It is certain neither secretary was Gestapo and this may just be a turn of phrase by Von Papen; he sometimes called Moyzisch a Gestapo man, thus the women working for him might be 'Gestapo'. Moyzisch's new secretary was called Cornelia Kapp.

Karl Kapp, Cornelia's father, met Seiler, who was staying at the Bulgari Hotel, reserved for Germans, during his visit to Sofia. Karl was an ardent supporter of the Nazi Party and worked at the German Legation as a diplomat. He asked Seiler about employment prospects for his daughter in Ankara, because Cornelia was highly strung and her nerves were frayed from the incessant air raids. He was concerned for his daughter and believed she would benefit from a rest in a neutral country.

Returning to Ankara, Seiler told Moyzisch about the Kapp girl; she was attractive and skilled in 'secretarial work', an 'excellent linguist' and, with her background, she was 'bound to be thoroughly reliable'.[4]

Moyzisch asked the ambassador if the Kapp girl would be acceptable to him. She was and Von Papen said he 'knew and respected her father'. Kapp was cleared to work in Ankara by the personnel department of the Foreign Ministry in Berlin, and, due to Operation Cicero, she also had to be passed by the RSHA. The reply was an offer to have a male secretary sent out from Berlin, but Moyzisch was dead set against it: 'I did not care for the idea of having one of Kaltenbrunner's stool pigeons sent to spy on me.' Kaltenbrunner did in the end relent, and Cornelia Kapp was transferred from Sofia to Ankara.[5]

Seiler and Moyzisch went to meet her at Ankara's station. Seiler hardly recognised her as the same person he had seen in Sofia, and Moyzisch's first reaction was of 'distinct shock'. Seiler described her as looking 'appalling' and a 'bundle of nerves'; she was a 'platinum blonde in her middle twenties', but now looked most unhealthy with 'a greyish tinge'.[6] It would appear from these descriptions of Cornelia Kapp that she had or was suffering some sort of nervous breakdown. Years later in an interview, Seiler said he felt: 'The girl seemed out of her mind.'[7]

They took her to a hotel, and then to Moyzisch's house where his wife had prepared a meal. Her manners and demeanour did not impress his wife. The next day she fell ill, and all Moyzisch could see was her 'face swelling in an alarming manner'. He called for a doctor. He also noticed she was taking sleeping pills, and thought her 'lackadaisical' manner might have been due to her abuse of sedatives.

Ten days after her arrival, the doctor pronounced her fit enough to work and she arrived at the office to start her new job. Far from being an asset, she had been an additional burden for Moyzisch, and her work proved 'thoroughly unsatisfactory' and 'full of mistakes'.[8]

Towards the end of January 1944, Moyzisch took his first leave since he had been in Turkey. He went to Brussa for a week, in the north-western part of Turkey on the Sea of Marmara (Marmara meaning 'marble' in Greek).[9] An important centre of the silk trade, on the old Silk Road east, it is well known for its thermal baths, rich fishing grounds and Mediterranean climate.

About the same time, Von Papen also went to Brussa where he 'hoped the mineral baths would relieve my rheumatism'.[10]

Moyzisch liked Brussa, commenting that it was a 'lovely city and one of the oldest in Turkey'.[11] It had been the capital of the Ottoman states in the fourteenth century and contained the mausoleums of the early Ottoman sultans. Over a thousand years before the city had been known to travellers as Prusa, named after King Prusias I of Bithynia, who founded the town in 183 BC. Both Germans no doubt looked forward to a quiet time, but things were not to turn out as they hoped.

Von Papen had been in Brussa barely a day when:

> A telephone call from Ankara put an end to my holiday.
>
> My visit was soon broken by the news brought to me by a member of my staff that one of our principal Abwehr agents in Istanbul, Dr Vermehren, had deserted to the British.[12]

Erich Vermehren was married to a remarkably courageous woman, Countess Elizabeth Plettenberg, a devout Catholic who had frequently risked imprisonment by the Nazis for distributing banned material, much of it Catholic criticism of the 'Pagan Nazis'. Elizabeth was also a cousin of Von Papen.

Erich had converted to the Catholic faith and worked with the Catholic underground movement against the Nazis; however, his resistance group in Germany had been infiltrated by a Gestapo agent. During a protracted investigation, countless members were implicated, including friends of the Vermehrens, and this is how he came to the attention of the SIS.[13]

It is little wonder Von Papen and Moyzisch hurried back to Ankara to face the fallout. Their absence from the embassy might be negatively interpreted by Berlin. It also did not help that the ambassador had helped Elizabeth obtain permission to leave Germany and join her husband in Istanbul, and there were people in Berlin who accused him of being involved in the defections.[14] Moyzisch was concerned with the effect the defection might have on Cicero: did the *Abwehr* know about Cicero; was his cover now blown? Also Moyzisch ran other agents that the Vermehren defection could affect.

The Vermehrens were not that big a catch, although the British propaganda machine went into overdrive to overplay their importance. Erich had already made one attempt to defect in Lisbon, but his wife had been forbidden to leave Germany by the Gestapo for several months. So he carried on with his modest duties alone in Istanbul, including making reports on British shipping movements.

Nicholas Elliot handled the SIS section in Istanbul; he had been the Section V representative in the city since the spring of 1942. Like Ankara,

Istanbul during the war years was a 'stew pot and counter-plot' by 'every power, every cause and every faith intrigued beside the Golden Horn'.[15]

Eric Newby said the city of Istanbul was '… still perhaps, apart from Peking, the most interesting and mysterious of the great cities of the world and from which, although still incomparable as a distant prospect, as it is to this day, much of the beauty had already long since melted away'.[16]

Elliot handled the Vermehrens with 'consummate skill and sympathy, but with just the necessary touch of firmness'. Vermehren's first approach was to the British assistant military attaché on 18 January at the Parc Hotel, a well-known haunt of most of the spies in the city. The military attaché, known as 'Cribb', passed him onto Elliot on 21 January; Vermehren said he was willing to work for SIS. Over a four-day period he photographed important *Abwehr* files, which recorded the complete *Abwehr* set up in Istanbul, Turkey and the Middle East. Before the end of January, Elliot was tipped off that the Turkish Secret Police knew Vermehren was working for the British, and it would not be long before the Germans would find out. The Vermehrens were smuggled out with two other *Abwehr* men to Cairo through the SIS station in Smyrna,[17] then via Gibraltar to Britain, where they took up residence in a South Kensington flat belonging to Kim Philby's mother.

The Vermehren family came from Lübeck, in northern Germany on the River Trave, and were ardently anti-Nazi. Erich's mother, Petra Vermehren, a renowned German journalist, was working in Portugal at the time and was ordered to return home to explain her son's defection. Johnny Jebsen, a friend of Erich's, known as 'Artist' by the British and working for them as a double agent within the *Abwehr*, tried to convince Petra not to return home but to defect. However, she would not and returned to Germany on the next plane to Berlin. She was well aware that, under the Nazi system of collective punishment, her fate was probably sealed.

She was arrested at the airport and sent to Sachsenhausen concentration camp. Her husband, son and two daughters were also arrested and sent to concentration camps. She survived Sachsenhausen, however, being liberated on 30 April 1945, after which she returned to her writing career.

Paul Leverkühn, the senior *Abwehr* officer in Turkey, was recalled to Berlin in disgrace. In the end the defection of a minor *Abwehr* officer and his wife had an effect far beyond their importance. The incident caused consternation in Germany and it marked the virtual demise of the *Abwehr* as an effective service; it was later taken over by the SD.

Hitler was furious and summoned Canaris to a meeting which would be the Admiral's last with the Führer. Did Hitler still harbour some hope for a deal with the West through Von Papen and the *Abwehr*? The Vermehrens' defection had the mark that 'the crew was abandoning ship' and Hitler told Canaris that his service was falling apart. The Admiral responded that is was 'hardly surprising given that Germany was losing the war'.[18] As a result, Hitler decided to put the *Abwehr* under the control of Himmler and Kaltenbrunner.

Two weeks later, Hitler set up a unified German intelligence service, something that Heydrich, while SS Chief of Intelligence, had argued for before his assassination. However, by the time Hitler put the wheels in motion, it was ill advised and far too late to make a difference.

Thus the service Canaris had built up over many years fell apart. Hundreds of officers and agents in important positions disappeared, resigned or applied for postings back to the armed forces; some would rather serve on the Russian front than under Himmler, Kaltenbrunner and Schellenberg. Canaris had been their much-respected leader and, even if they found his 'excessive scruples' tiresome, 'they knew it was him they had to thank for being able to keep their hands clean from the mire and blood in which Germany was foundering'.[19]

Schellenberg had a high regard for Canaris, and found him a 'highly intelligent and sensitive man with many likeable qualities'. He knew the *Abwehr* would disintegrate without him, and the SD was not up to the task of taking over. The decision could not have come at a worse time with the Allied landings looming in the west. But there was little Schellenberg could do to save the *Abwehr* network in the Low Countries and France.[20]

Von Papen tried to obtain a reversal of Hitler's decree on the *Abwehr*, but found:

My own position in Berlin had been considerably weakened and the party was clamouring for me to be brought to trial. I was to learn later that the Gestapo made plans about this time to send a plane-load of reliable SS men in plain clothes to Ankara for the purpose of kidnapping me and taking me back to Berlin. Apparently Hitler did not permit this in the end, although Ribbentrop had already signified his approval of the scheme.[21]

Moyzisch had been friendly with Leverkühn and was distressed that his future now 'hung on a very thin thread indeed'. However, these events did bring Cornelia Kapp out of herself; she became passionate and vocal about traitors, confiding to him: 'she could not understand how any German could go over to the enemy while his country was engaged in a life and death struggle' and this type of behaviour was 'despicable'.[22]

She went on to tell him about her two brothers who were officers serving at the front. Yet Moyzisch says he was never really happy with her. Was this a comment with the benefit of hindsight, for Moyzisch went to a lot of trouble to try and make her feel at home. Maybe it was out of respect for her father, Karl, although it was Von Papen who knew him and not Moyzisch:

> Yet there was always something strange about her. It was difficult not to be irritated by her sudden fits of looking and behaving as though she was so utterly bored. Many times at parties I saw a group of cheerfully chattering people fall silent as Elisabet [Cornelia] approached.[23]

Cicero first talked to her when he telephoned Moyzisch's office as 'Pierre'. He says he flirted with her on the line and she asked him 'who he really was', but he avoided any answer.

Moyzisch and Cicero met at the corner of Ozchemir Street in the Guzelyurt area of the city that night. They drove around the old city's dimly lit streets in the Opel Admiral conducting their business.

Cicero said, 'Your secretary told me she is going on leave at Easter.'

Moyzisch replied he would be glad of that, and it was apparent he was not pleased with his new assistant. Cicero goaded him by saying he would like a date with her.

Moyzisch said that, if he liked 'hysterical women' then he was welcome to do so. He was in a black mood observed Cicero, who was in high spirits.

In fact, he was so confident that he had even gone back to hiding the money under the carpet in his room again at the embassy. He may not have been so happy had he known who Cornelia Kapp really was, and that she had begun looking for him.[24]

## 15

# CICERO'S LATER PERIOD

By the end of January 1944 Cicero had been paid some £200,000 (about £4.5 million today). The British investigation, despite his bluster, had curtailed his deliveries for a while and it is curious as to why he did not give up the enterprise.

Moyzisch asked himself the very same question; after all, Cicero had enough money to keep him in luxury for life. But he felt it was the feeling of 'power' that acted on him like an addictive drug.[1] Bazna confirms this by saying he felt showing off to Esra gave him a buzz: 'The thrill of playing with danger held me in its grip … I thought that things would go on like this forever'.[2]

At the start of February Cicero resumed his work. He, too, had been concerned about the fallout from the Vermehrens' defection. About this time he met Moyzisch again at his office, as the SD man was extremely busy, and he used the same approach route through the hole in the fence behind the tool shed. He was received by Herr Jenke this time, who told him Moyzisch would soon be there. They briefly talked about the likelihood of Turkey entering the war, at which point Jenke told Bazna that, when the war was over, Hitler intended to present him with a villa in Germany in gratitude for his work for the Fatherland. Bazna found this prospect 'highly pleasing to my self esteem'.[3]

Some have suggested Bazna may well have invented this story to embellish his standing. However, by this stage in the war, his importance to Germany would surely have risen due to the loss of so many *Abwehr* connections. Von Papen had alerted Ribbentrop that they might soon lose Cicero too.[4]

Cicero kept delivering material, but Moyzisch observed that 'it was nowhere near his former standard' and his access to documents was now more dependent on luck.

Assuming that payment remained at £10,000 per roll, Moyzisch sent in a statement to Berlin towards the end of February and the total paid had risen to £300,000, which meant Cicero would have delivered at least another ten rolls in this last period.[5]

It is hard to say just how many photographs Cicero took, or the total number of rolls of film he delivered. Maria Molkenteller believed she translated 130–150 telegrams.[6] Were these documents filtered before she received them? No copies of the documents were ever found.[7] Moyzisch thought the total was around 'four hundred photographs'.[8]

By the middle of February, Von Papen wrote that:

The British had realised at last that there was no way of overcoming Turkish opposition to taking part in the war, and the whole Balkan operation had to be abandoned.[9]

It was certainly true that relations between Britain and Turkey had reached their lowest point, yet Von Papen was wise enough to know that this situation would not last. He entertained the Turkish Cabinet at the embassy with a concert by the pianist Walter Gieseking on 8 February, where Menemencioglu 'made no attempt to disguise his disquiet at the situation and told me that Turkey could not allow her relations with her British and American Allies to get worse'.[10]

He knew he was in a weak position with Germany's declining power, but he still tried to use his influence in Ankara to hinder any new alignment. He also hoped that Cicero's information might aid Germany's military policies, but Berlin largely failed to recognise the opportunity before them.

OKW received much information from the Cicero documents and the chief of staff, General Alfred Jodl, confided to his diary that the British position in the Balkans now held little threat.[11] The Allies were preparing for a spring invasion of Western Europe and, therefore, troops from the Balkans could be released to other fronts.

In February it was suggested two divisions could be transferred to France or Italy. The movement of these troops was delayed, however, as 'Hitler did not trust the intelligence reports'.[12] He felt he needed to keep the Balkans in check and removing troops would send the wrong message. There were also vital supplies needed from this region, including oil, to be considered. The Cicero documents were used by Hitler and

Ribbentrop to reassure the nervous leaders of Bulgaria and Hungary that the Allies proposed no immediate invasion of the Balkans through Turkey. Nevertheless, the promises became hollow when, in March, the Red Army's new offensive in the Ukraine threatened the entire region, and all units were needed to try and halt the drive. The British aim of tying down German forces in the Balkans had been achieved, albeit by the advance of Soviet forces.

During this late period, Cicero and Moyzisch claimed they discovered details of Operation Overlord, the Allied invasion of Western Europe. When Moyzisch discovered Overlord was the likely codename for the invasion, he straight away signalled Berlin 'giving my theory'. Apparently they replied a week later, saying, 'Possible but hardly probable'.[13] Cicero claimed he was 'the first person on the other side who knew about 'Operation Overlord',[14] but this is highly unlikely as Maria Molkenteller, in her interrogation by SIS, stated the RSHA knew about 'Operation Overlord' as early as November 1943, albeit with few details.[15]

Was the codename 'Overlord' all that Cicero revealed? Surely this would certainly have turned up in other reports. But Cicero also points to General Eisenhower being appointed to command the operation. Is this Bazna using the benefit of hindsight? Moyzisch says he told Cicero that, for any reference he overheard to 'Overlord', he was to 'memorise the exact context and report to me'. Although he appeared 'quite uninterested and merely shrugged his shoulders. As usual it was no use giving him orders.'[16]

Moyzisch also found the date 15 May 1944 in a Cicero document, a signal from London to the British ambassador, insisting 'Anglo-Turkish negotiations must be completed' by that date. He reasoned why. Was this another reference to 'Overlord'? The invasion took place on 6 June but it had been planned for May. Or did the date refer to something totally different?

General Jodl believed the codename 'Overlord', the likely invasion from Britain, had come from Cicero. Nicholas Elliot, head of SIS Section V in Istanbul, says he and Sir Hughe both knew the Overlord date to be 4–5 June, and waited in the embassy for reports on the landings.[17]

At the Tehran conference, a number of important decisions for the conduct of the war were taken, including the 'approximate date and location of Overlord'.[18] The codename 'Overlord' had been the name for the invasion since September 1943, but later, at the insistence of the

British, it became the codename for the overall Anglo–American strategy in North Western Europe. The invasion codename was then changed to 'Neptune'. The Germans learned little about the key secrets of D-Day and were utterly deceived as to its timing and whereabouts.[19]

Moyzisch says Cicero's last documents contained the codename 'Operation Overlord', but he was despondent:

> It seems ironic that the last piece of invaluable information supplied by Cicero should have been treated by Berlin with exactly the same lack of comprehension as all the others.[20]

# 16

# ANOTHER SPY

It is striking just how many women through history have made good spies. Just when Cornelia Kapp became an American spy is hard to pinpoint, but she claims to have already been recruited before she arrived at Ankara station in 'a most unattractive' state. She was to be met by Moyzisch and Seiler. Was this a ruse? If so, then it would seem to have been an elaborate one.[1]

It was Hans Nogly, the man who helped Bazna with his book, who found out much of the background details about Cornelia Kapp, with the help of the journalist G. Thomas Beyl. Moyzisch fails to even mention her espionage.

Born in Berlin on 31 July 1919, Cornelia says she was 6 years old when her parents first took her to the United States. Her father, Karl Kapp, worked in the diplomatic service in Bombay, before being moved to the United States, where he became Consul General at Cleveland, Ohio. He also worked for the *Abwehr* from as early as 1938. He sent detailed reports via the diplomatic pouch from Washington on information gained by his agents about factories being converted from civilian use to war production.[2]

Cornelia says she made all her friends in America, so it must have been a wrench for her to leave, and the Kapps remained there until just before war broke out between the USA and Germany in 1941. While in Cleveland she fell in love with a young American, who she would later meet again when he was working in intelligence.[3]

Returning to Germany, she was trained as a nurse in Stuttgart. This was not a calling for her, but rather a way to avoid 'work in a factory'. However, after her father pulled some strings, she joined her parents after they were posted to Italy.

In July 1943, a new posting took the Kapps to Sofia, where Karl joined the German diplomatic mission, and Cornelia worked as a secretary and translator at the German Embassy. Within a month, she was approached by the OSS 'and I engaged in espionage work for the Americans in Sofia'.[4]

When her father asked Seiler about jobs in Ankara, it was due to her nervous state during air raids. If, as she says, she was recruited in Sofia, it was before she or the OSS knew about her transfer to Turkey.[5] So she was no deliberate plant – it was more that opportunity presented itself in Ankara; she may well have worked on similar openings in Sofia, and as mentioned she said she was 'engaged in espionage work for the Americans' there.[6] The Americans may well have seen her transfer to the German Embassy in Ankara as a golden opportunity, and briefed her about Cicero before she left.[7]

However, the CIA/OSS files paint a different picture. The Americans call Cornelia 'Nele Kapp', obviously a shortened version, and say she was not approached by them in Sofia.[8] She first made contact via a German Jewish dentist in Ankara, known to be a source of contacts, and she asked him to put her in touch with the Americans. She met a US Foreign Service officer at the dentist and told him she was willing to obtain information for them, and, in return, she wanted them to get her out of Turkey to America.

Her offer went to the US ambassador, Laurence A. Steinhardt, and the reply was: 'The Americans will promise nothing, but we will be glad to receive the information. If she cares to take it on that basis that's fine'. The Nele affair was then turned over to the American military attaché.[9]

Over a number of weeks Nele made 'a fairly full report on Moyzisch's activities', including lists of spies working in the Middle East. And she also revealed that a man who called himself 'Cicero' contacted the embassy and that it had something to do with the British. When the man phoned 'everybody was shooed out of the place'. Steinhardt indicated the British should be told, yet it would appear they were not informed by the OSS in Ankara until much later.[10]

Kapp's actions in betraying her country may explain why she often asked Moyzisch about the war situation and deserters: 'Do you think Germany can still win the war?' Was the position 'bad on all fronts?' As would be expected, Moyzisch's replies tried to paint a brighter picture.[11]

In Ankara, Cornelia says her work was easy at the German Embassy, and in four days she had the key to Moyzisch's safe and he 'fell for all my play-acting'. She also says she met her old lover from Cleveland, who was working for OSS.[12]

As far as the mysterious agent Cicero was concerned, she says:

I knew about Cicero before it became my task to open the mail that arrived in the German Embassy every evening by courier from Berlin. As I worked alone and undisturbed, I had plenty of time to copy out documents from Berlin which made it clear that Cicero was to be sought in the British Embassy itself. I handed over the copies to the Americans every evening. The Americans once nearly caught sight of the man who used often to meet Moyzisch in the evening and always jumped into his car. That was on the evening when Moyzisch and Cicero only just managed to get away after the wild car chase through the whole of Ankara.[13]

Her mission was now to 'establish his identity'. Bazna says he spoke to Moyzisch's new secretary as 'Pierre' on the telephone several times, and that she had a 'bright, pleasant voice'. Yet in her interrogation by MI6 in Cairo, Cornelia said, 'Cicero never rang up while she was there except on a Monday in the latter part of March', and that she knew the conversations were in French and would be inviting Moyzisch to play 'bridge or poker'.[14]

Cornelia says that once, while watching Moyzisch's rooms at night, she thinks she saw a shadowy figure, but he 'went off quickly in the direction of the tool shed in the garden, and by the time I reached the spot he had vanished'.[15]

Shortly before Cornelia defected to the Americans, she went to the ABC store with Moyzisch to buy some lingerie. He had given her a lift into the town, and she had asked him for help as her Turkish was not good, so reluctantly he went with her. While in the shop he noticed Cicero enter. The two men ignored each other, and Moyzisch later recorded that Cicero ordered 'expensive silk shirts' and he recalled thinking 'such childish ostentation would be the end of him yet'.

Bazna felt the look he got from Moyzisch was 'cordially wishing me in hell'. But he had eyes only for the attractive girl he was with, with her 'auburn hair, her long legs, her eyes' – he was captivated.

Even Moyzisch's knowledge of Turkish was not up to the intrigues of ordering lingerie, the more so as she wanted the 'underclothes made to measure'. So Bazna stepped forward and offered to act as their interpreter; he spoke to them in French, and he explained to the sales assistant what was required. Moyzisch says he felt 'uncomfortable' and stayed out of the conversation. Cornelia was enjoying the whole experience, being the centre of attention and laughing at the situation.

Her measurements were taken while the men looked the other way. Bazna asked her if she was German and said he hoped she was enjoying her time in Ankara. Then, with a 'huge roll' of notes, Moyzisch says Bazna paid for his shirts. Bazna bowed to Cornelia, and while no one was watching he turned to Moyzisch and gave him 'a broad wink'.

Cornelia also recalled the meeting at the ABC and remembered a man helping me in 'choosing underwear'. And that he was 'amusing to talk to'. However, she could not recognise him as Cicero, never having seen Cicero other than as a fleeting glimpse of a shadowy figure.[16] Bazna revealed he was in the ABC at the time to buy a dress as a surprise for Esra, who had seen it in the window display and admired it. Seiler said he, too, knew about Moyzisch's and Cornelia's visit to the ABC.

In his account, Moyzisch never admitted to Kapp ever being a spy, but he did reveal security lapses that could have been taken advantage of. In March the reliable Schnurchen went down with 'flu'. The workload was heavy but, to his surprise, Kapp rose to the occasion: 'she worked very hard, and far more conscientiously than usual.' The day with the most demands was the one before the courier plane left for Berlin.

They had to work late into the night on the day before the delivery, and Kapp even volunteered to stay on and finish the work. Moyzisch went home, leaving Kapp with the safe key. But he could not rest and returned to the office about midnight; she was still there working and he could see her through the window as she had not drawn the curtains. He told her to go home and he locked the safe and retained the key.[17] She complained he did not trust her as Schnurchen was 'allowed to keep the key'. He told her this was not the case, and she had had the key for several hours. It was merely that he slept better if he had the key with him.[18]

Towards the end of March, Moyzisch says 'Elisabet [Cornelia] learned about Operation Cicero'. He was in Istanbul when the diplomatic bag arrived at the embassy. As she was the only one in the department, she opened the letters. Usually things referring to 'Cicero' were in envelopes marked for Moyzisch and he opened them, but, on this occasion, they were not marked for him, so she opened them. On his return she asked him who 'Cicero' was. He replied that this was a matter he would deal with alone. However, the letters she had seen with no explanation 'made it quite clear ... that Operation Cicero referred to something going on inside the British Embassy'.[19]

With the return of Schnurchen to work, Kapp went back to her more mundane office work, and the standard of that work dropped off again. Moyzisch lost his temper with a poor translation she produced, suggesting that, if her work did not improve, it would be better for all concerned if she went back to her 'old job in Sofia'.[20]

About this time Moyzisch says Kapp approached him about finding her friend, Hans, a *Luftwaffe* man, some work. He had heard of this man before; back in September, there were two he called Hans and Fritz, who said they had been shot down over the Black Sea by Russian aircraft. Having reached neutral Turkey, they were interned. The Turks did not put foreign nationals in this position behind bars, but accommodated them in Ankara hotels and allowed them broad freedom in the city under parole. These two flyers were well treated by the German community in Ankara, and were popular with the ladies:

> Hans and Fritz were given a very good time, lunching and dining out on their heroic exploits of the past, no less than on their ardent hopes for the future.

Later, it was revealed by *Luftwaffe* sources that these two were likely deserters, and might have even been on the 'payroll of the British Secret Service'.

A *Luftwaffe* investigation found these two had taken off on a test flight from an airfield in the Crimea and had never been seen again. But this was long after 'Operation Cicero' had begun and Moyzisch had never met them:[21]

> She was evidently anxious to help the young men, and of course I remembered the gossip I had heard about her having an affair with one of them. I agreed to see him.'[22]

During her interrogation, Kapp told MI6 that she met her German lover at the house of 'Some Americans in Ankara' and one can assume that this was likely to have been an OSS safe house.[23]

The day after Kapp's request, the two flyers turned up in the SD office. It was largely a waste of time as far as Moyzisch was concerned: they smoked his cigarettes and talked a lot. No doubt he hoped to learn something to his advantage, but he did not. Once they had finished, he told them there was no work for them as no one could be taken on, even unpaid, without Foreign Ministry permission. They left his office frustrated, and Kapp made it obvious to Moyzisch that she felt let down, believing he was merely using the Foreign Ministry as an excuse.[24]

Shortly after this, at a dinner party held at Moyzisch's home, she turned up late, 'nervous' and 'pale'. She ate and drank little. Later, it was revealed she thought they were going to poison her. Seiler felt Kapp had become 'a specialist in nervous breakdowns' and that she also used letters from her brothers to draw attention to her nervous state. She read the letters aloud at the office: 'They were very moving. The kind of things soldiers write when trying to make sense of war ...'[25] Moyzisch said to Seiler that, after reading them, she had 'a fit of uncontrollable sobbing at her desk'. He also felt she was so often in a poor state that he 'wanted to get rid of her'.[26]

Moyzisch went to Von Papen to discuss the Kapp situation, but the ambassador was not keen to get rid of her, commenting that, after all the trouble they had taken to obtain her posting, this would reflect badly on them.

But Moyzisch felt she was too much of a distraction with the burden of Operation Cicero. Von Papen pointed out that, if they said she was no good, then she would be sent back to Germany to work in a factory, and they had to consider her father in all this, a personal friend of Von Papen. They agreed to contact her father and tell him she was ill, and he could come and collect her. As far as Berlin was concerned, she was on sick leave and 'gone for treatment', which, after all, they felt was not far from the truth.[27]

Herr Kapp replied to Von Papen, reporting that he had been transferred to Budapest during a recent crisis. German troops had moved en masse into Hungary in the third week of March; the wavering government there had been removed after bad German reverses in the east. Ten divisions of the Eighth Army had been trapped south-east of Kiev and 60,000 German troops had been lost. As a consequence, he could not leave Budapest until Easter.

However, Cornelia was to act first, guided by her American friends. On Monday 3 April she approached Moyzisch and asked for 'a few days leave over Easter'. She wanted to spend a week with her parents in Budapest, and one of her brothers would be there on leave.[28] Moyzisch could hardly believe his luck and was delighted at the request. Once in Budapest her father could keep her there. He did not give in right away, trying not to make it too obvious, and he pointed out the pressures of work and the shortage of staff. But she promised to get all the work done by Thursday.

So it was agreed: she would catch the Istanbul train on Thursday evening and the courier plane to Budapest the next day. They even agreed she would return on 12 April, but, of course, neither of them had any intention of this happening. A letter would travel in a diplomatic bag on the train and plane to Budapest, indicating Cornelia was to stay with her parents, as her services were no longer required in Ankara. Or that's what the man from the SD thought would happen, but Cornelia had other plans.[29]

# 17

# TWO SPIES BOW OUT

Was the man Bazna was to call Sears a figment of his imagination or, as he says, 'a British agent'? He says he saw him with Cornelia Kapp at the Ankara Palace Hotel – and they were talking intimately in the lounge. It was the hall porter who told him the man's name was Sears or 'something of the sort' and he was English. Bazna thought he resembled the driver of the car during the chase – the man with the 'smooth face' – but he got only the briefest glimpse of him. However, all this seems unlikely. Whatever happened, at this point Bazna was in a panic – he saw enemy agents everywhere.[1]

One source indicates that Cornelia Kapp was controlled by an OSS agent called Ewart Seager, who may even have been the Cleveland man that she later married. Conversely, another source suggests she had an affair with the OSS man in Sofia, while later in the United States she married an FBI agent.[2]

Bazna was shocked and afraid: who was this girl? And which side was she working for? He tried to contact Moyzisch, but he was not at the embassy. He acted quickly, removing all the money from under the carpet in his room at the British Embassy and taking it with the camera to his house. There he destroyed all his camera equipment and threw it 'into the Incesu Deresi, which is a small river'. He packed all the money at the house into a suitcase, though most of the money was now at a bank 'deposit safe'.

He remained restless and woke Esra at 4 a.m., telling her to meet him near the British Embassy at midday in a taxi with the suitcase; they would then take it to the bank. He told her to pack everything she needed, for they would not return to the house.

'She tried to remain calm, but her whole body was trembling.' He told her to take a room in a hotel; he would take care of everything. He reassured her 'nothing had happened', and that he had simply decided to bring his brief espionage career to an end.[3]

On the morning of Cornelia Kapp's departure, Thursday 6 April, she came to Moyzisch's office to say goodbye to him and Schnurchen, who she promised to bring back a 'delicious Hungarian Easter Egg'. Moyzisch said he would see her off at the station as he 'had left her ticket at home', though he just 'wanted to make sure she actually went'.[4]

Kapp says she felt the very real danger of being caught at this juncture. The Americans had given her some poison 'to provide for all emergencies' and she knew full well what awaited her in Germany if she was uncovered. She had done all she could in providing all 'the information about Cicero that it was possible to obtain', along with other material, such as the 'German diplomatic secret cipher'. The Americans came up with the idea of her asking for Easter leave.[5]

At 5.30 p.m. on the Thursday, Moyzisch was waiting at the station for the overnight train to leave for Istanbul. The train was already standing at the platform, its locomotive gently omitting steam and smoke, as if resting before the long haul west to the Golden Horn. As usual he had to bribe the booking clerk to get Cornelia a seat, but there was no sign of her as yet.

Von Papen was also at the station, saying goodbye to the Spanish ambassador who was leaving Ankara on the same train. Moyzisch stayed out of their way, walking up and down the square in front of the station. His frustration rising, he wondered why she could not 'be punctual'. The thought occurred to him that he had missed her in the crowd and she was already on the train, but she was not there either.

With five minutes to go his nervousness became palpable as thoughts raced through his mind. At this point, Von Papen, having said his farewell to his Spanish colleague, approached Moyzisch and asked where his secretary was. The SD man said he did not know.

'She'll probably turn up just as the train is pulling out. Some women are like that,' said Von Papen before he left.[6]

Moyzisch watched the train leave without her. On board with the courier was the diplomatic bag with a letter for her father. He drove from the station to her flat. Her flatmate opened the door and told him Cornelia was gone, with all her clothes and possessions packed in trunks and a suitcase. Her room was bare, other than an old coat she had discarded. Moyzisch had no idea where she might be, but felt that she must be somewhere in Ankara. He must have been consumed with dread, for her actions were not those of someone going to return after the Easter holidays. But he pushed these feelings to the back of his mind and considered the next step.

Cornelia says she went to the American house and the OSS man 'I had known since my Cleveland days'. Her main motive was not her love affair with the American, but her 'desire to return to America, and that was promised me as the reward for my espionage work ... I was never paid for what I did'.[7]

In Von Papen's office, Moyzisch told him what he had discovered. He had never seen the ambassador so angry, and he was blamed for taking on such a neurotic woman. The SD man said he would go and look for her, and if he could not find her he would inform Berlin and the Turkish Police. Von Papen agreed but requested a further meeting, since they must try to avoid a scandal at all costs.

Moyzisch toured Ankara in his car looking wherever he thought she might be. He even went to the hotel of the two flyers, who were both angry at being roused from their beds, but they had not seen her for days. He phoned the consulate in Istanbul and arranged for someone to meet the Ankara train in case somehow she was on it. He then went back to the station and searched the next train for Adana, but found nothing.

Returning home he rested and thought more clearly. There were only two possibilities: either she had been in an accident or she had deserted. The evidence of her taking all her belongings certainly pointed to the latter:

> In that case it meant ruin for me and possibly even death; a concentration camp, almost certainly.[8]

The next morning he went back to Cornelia's flat to find she had not returned there. However, he did learn that a junior secretary at the British Embassy also lived in the same block; a fact which did not improve his mood.

A friend at the Turkish Foreign Ministry told Moyzisch that there were no reports of an accident involving a German woman, or suicide. In his opinion, therefore, she must have deserted. Back in his own office he was informed by the consulate in Istanbul that his secretary was not on the train from Ankara either:

> I had no choice now. Berlin must be informed. I drafted the most difficult signal of my life, reporting that my secretary had vanished without trace, and that while the possibilities of suicide or accident could not yet be ruled out it was equally possible that she had deserted to the British.[9]

Bazna heard of the defection of Cornelia Kapp on the Ankara grapevine. He even says that Sir Hughe told him of her defection and that: 'The whole Papen household is upside down.' Yet he was not even sure it was the same person. Did Bazna connect the occurrence with the young blonde woman he had taken a fancy to at the ABC, and seen again at the Palace Hotel? Or was he just imagining things?[10]

Nothing had happened since he had left his house. Esra had a room in the old city, where he had stored all his expensive clothes, and the money was safe in the bank. The only thing that really alarmed him was that he could not contact Moyzisch. He had telephoned many times, but the SD man was not available. He had the feeling something was going on, and it would not be good for him.

The defection was common knowledge below stairs at the British Embassy and the chef, Manoli Filoti, told him that a woman had 'deserted from the German Embassy'. This gossip was not unusual as Turks worked as domestic servants in all the embassies in Ankara; they knew each other and bartered goods for their masters, and thus Scotch whisky flowed freely at the German Embassy and Hock at the British Embassy. The chef even knew her name: 'She's a secretary named Cornelia Kapp.' Bazna says this was the first time he heard the name, although it meant nothing to him.

At afternoon tea in Sir Hughe's room, Mr Busk was with the ambassador and Bazna says he walked in on their conversation: '... flown to Cairo. She is being thoroughly interrogated'. Then he says they immediately changed the subject, although this seems overly convenient.

Shortly after, Bazna says he spotted Sears waiting outside the British Embassy and, when the latter walked away and got into a taxi on Ataturk Boulevard, he followed him. Bazna took another, instructing the driver to 'follow that cab'. They stopped at a block of flats and Sears paid off the taxi. Then Bazna spent his time watching the flats, but nothing happened.

While doing this he says he virtually bumped into Sears, this time with a woman in the uniform of a British WRNS officer with short black hair. However, when they walked away Bazna says he recognised 'her gait, the way she held herself'. He felt she must be Cornelia Kapp.[11]

The Americans had housed Cornelia with two American girls, secretaries at the US Embassy, for a week. Here her hair was changed from ash blonde to black, and she had to hide under the bed if anybody called. The girl who dyed Cornelia's hair could not remove the dye from her hands, so had to stay off work. Her boss came to see her the next day with roses while Cornelia hid under the bed. Finally, it took petrol to remove the dye.

The OSS went to some lengths to conceal the movement of Cornelia. The northbound and southbound trains came into Ankara station at the same time, remaining there about five to ten minutes. A few miles west of Ankara, the northbound (Istanbul) train stopped at Ayash; it was even possible to miss the train at Ankara, but beat it to Ayash in a car and catch it there. The southbound train went on into Syria and Iraq. Under the guise of an outing, several Americans from the embassy went to the girl's apartment, and then went to Ayash with Cornelia among them. While at Ankara station, another group boarded the southbound train and then, at the last minute, switched to the northbound (Istanbul) train, just as it was leaving. They hoped this would leave any followers on the wrong train.

At Ayash station Cornelia joined the Istanbul train, which involved bribing the conductor and inventing a story about newlyweds so they would not to be disturbed; an OSS agent was already on board and would act as her bridegroom. Money, nods and winks were exchanged.[12]

The OSS man gave her a loaded gun and also laced her with a 'thick slug of straight scotch'. Then they lay down on the bunks, Cornelia on the upper berth. During the night she had to go to the bathroom several times to be sick, insisting the OSS man went outside: 'I'll knock on the door when you can come in again.' He complied with her wishes, smiling at the conductor while he waited for the knock. They left the train at 6 a.m. and, as they were leaving, the conductor told the OSS man not to worry as brides were '… often like that the first night'.

However, they did not go to Istanbul, but continued with the carriages taken off for Balikesir, which was near to a British camp and largely manned by the RAF. There the 'newlyweds' were met by the British and taken to the camp to spend the night. The next day a truck took them to Izmir, and there they waited for a caique coming in from Greece. That night the boat took her to Cyprus, where a plane then took her to Cairo.[13]

The next day, Bazna finally managed to get through to Moyzisch. He says he met the SD man in the old way, in his office, through the embassy grounds via the gap in the fence past the tool shed, but Moyzisch places this meeting in a friend's flat, maybe Seiler's, which is more likely given the situation.

There are other differences in their memories. Moyzisch says Cicero was anxious and he 'had been biting his nails again'. Bazna recalled that the SD man 'looked ill' and that he had developed a facial twitch.[14]

Cicero told Moyzisch that he was giving up spying, as he knew it was his secretary, the one he had spoken to on the phone and seen him with at the ABC, who had gone over to the British, and that she was called Cornelia Kapp.

The SD man admitted they did not know where she had gone.

'She's still in Ankara,' said Bazna, and wrote down the address of the flats near the Marmara Sokagi where he had spotted her. 'What does she know about me?'

Moyzisch did not really know; his codename for certain, perhaps more. He told Cicero to 'get out of Ankara just as fast as you can'.

Cicero told him his secretary was no longer blonde but now brunette and that her hair had been cut short. He also requested money that he was owed, which Moyzisch took from the safe.

To Moyzisch, Cicero looked a 'beaten man'. For the first and last time they shook hands. Moyzisch says his grip was limp.

'*Au revoir, Monsieur,*' said Cicero.

Of the spy known as Cicero, Moyzisch wrote that he 'quickly walked out of the house and vanished into the darkness. I never saw him again.'[15]

Back at the British Embassy, Bazna says he handed in his notice to Sir Hughe and told him that he was returning to Istanbul and his family. At first glance this would seem unlikely, but it may have been a way to cover his tracks. He says he 'did not want to spoil this last chance of living a life of luxury'.

Sir Hughe told him to 'settle things with Zeki', the butler, who would take over his duties. He says he left the British Embassy on the last day of April 1944, although it is likely he would have gone before that. He tells us he tried to say goodbye to Sir Hughe, but Zeki told him the ambassador was far too busy to see him.

He left the embassy with a few possessions in a 'cardboard attaché case' by the servant's entrance onto Ahmet Agaoglu Street. The street was 'empty' and he went 'unnoticed by anyone, a short, thickset man, beginning to grow bald'. He walked away into history, his importance yet to be revealed.[16]

# 18

# THE FALLOUT

Cornelia Kapp says of her interrogation:

> Prior to that time the British had had no suspicion of Cicero's existence.
> The American Secret Service wanted to present their British colleagues
> with a fait accompli. I was flown to Cairo and presented to the British,
> and it was in Cairo that the British for the first time heard the name of
> Cicero from the Americans, who presented me as evidence.[1]

This, of course, is not true, even if she thought it was; the British knew of
Cicero from January 1944, as they had been warned by the Fritz Kolbe
documents, 'a most secret source'.[2]

At first she was interned in a prisoner-of-war camp, which made her
angry and ill-disposed to the British.[3] She says her interrogators listened
to her with 'expressionless faces. I have no idea whether they believed
me or not.'[4]

This presents a rather different picture from the interrogation notes
of 30 May 1944. For a start Cornelia told her interrogators that she had
been ordered 'to return to Germany', which was why 'she fled to her
American friends'. Rather than saying her nerve had gone, the OSS had
already told her to minimise their role in the affair. The British found her
hysterical and 'lavishly drugged with luminal,' a barbiturate prescribed as
a sedative to relieve anxiety. It also has hypnotic properties and it took
them some time just to calm her down.

She described working for Moyzisch, and said Klaus Von Muhler and
Hugo (more probably Julius) Seiler worked closely with the SD man. She
mentioned a 'travelling agent nicknamed Cicero', but here the information was described as 'meagre'. Similarly, the documents she brought with
her were 'either too brief or too vague to be of major importance'.[5]

She was employed in a far less responsible and confidential position than the deserters who came across to us 3 months ago, and her contribution to our knowledge of German organisation and activities cannot be compared to theirs.[6]

Here they refer to the Vermehren defections of January and the important *Abwehr* files that they handed over, which contained information on the German set up in Istanbul and details of operations in Turkey and the Middle East.

At the end of May, Cornelia Kapp was released to the Americans and was sent to the United States, where she lived in Elizabeth, New Jersey, until the end of the war.[7]

★★★

Things did not go so well for Moyzisch after Kapp's defection. He had reluctantly informed Berlin and was soon overwhelmed by an 'avalanche of excited signals' asking questions he had no answers to.

Five days after Kapp's disappearance, he received an order from Kaltenbrunner's office to report to Berlin at once on the next courier plane. Like a condemned man, he dutifully took the night train to Istanbul on 12 April, and the plane was due to leave two days later.

In Istanbul he visited the consulate to see if there was any mail for him. There were more messages from Kaltenbrunner and the Foreign Ministry, both blaming him for the Kapp disappearance. There was also a personal letter for him, from a friend at the Foreign Ministry, advising him he would certainly be arrested as soon as he was on German soil, and to avoid any return at all costs.[8] He was in a dilemma over what to do. Eventually he decided he would feign illness and tell Berlin that his doctor had advised him not to travel.

While in his hotel room in Istanbul, he says he got several telephone calls from the British, encouraging him to defect. However, he felt unable to go that far for most of his family still lived in Germany. The British were persistent. He bribed the hotel switchboard operator not to put the calls through to his room. This worked briefly, but they started again as, no doubt, the British had upped their bribe. In the end, to get some peace, he cut the telephone line.[9]

The next day the courier plane took off for Berlin, while Moyzisch booked the night train to Ankara. He had to pay five times the going rate to get a sleeper. It was an awful journey and he got little sleep, no doubt wrestling with his dilemma.

Arriving back in Ankara he updated Von Papen, who told him to rest. In his office he found nothing missing from the safe, but that did not mean Cornelia had not copied documents. Did she use a camera? The irony of the situation seems to have escaped him. His hair was turning grey around the temples, he had a constant headache and he was running a temperature. There were no further messages from Berlin, and he found the 'silence ominous'. Returning to his home he took to his bed.[10]

After two weeks, during which time Cicero had been trying to contact him, he tentatively returned to work. A few days later, the two airmen visited him again on 'instructions from the British', but he would not listen. Another man he had known for many years also asked him to meet the British, but Moyzisch told him he was wasting his time and he 'would never desert to the enemy'.

News arrived from Berlin that an enquiry had been started in his absence, 'to establish the extent to which you are guilty of aiding and abetting your secretary's desertion to the enemy on 6 April'. Moyzisch was able to avoid returning to Germany while the Nazis were in power, using delays and major events turning against Germany to stay in Turkey.[11]

Von Papen spent Easter 1944 in Istanbul:

Odessa had fallen, the siege of the Crimea had begun, and we were greatly worried about my daughter, Isabelle, who had just left for Bucharest on her way back to nursing duties in a field hospital in the area.[12]

In April Von Papen was informed by Menemencioglu that, with regret, Turkey would be suspending deliveries of supplies of chromium ore to Germany. He was ordered to report back to Germany by Ribbentrop. The flight was 'unpleasant' having to fly 'over the Black Sea, Bulgaria, and Yugoslavia more or less at ground level, in order to avoid Allied air attacks'. The Turkish government was told the ambassador would not return to Ankara for the time being, an action tantamount to breaking off diplomatic relations.

Von Papen advised Ribbentrop that such action would only please the Allies, driving Turkey further into their camp, and he offered his resignation in protest. Ribbentrop declined the offer, saying this was a matter for Hitler. The Führer was not in favour of tough measures against Turkey, as they were in no position to carry them out, and thought it better to have an ambassador back at his post in Ankara – a snub for Ribbentrop.

The Cicero documents were also discussed and, in particular, the 'Tehran decisions'. Hitler felt it was a ploy to 'inject the idea of capitulation'. And he was convinced that the 'Atlantic Wall was impregnable'. Once the Allies had been thrown back, the Germans would beat the Russians. Von Papen felt there was 'little point in going on with the conversation', for the others present also refused to recognise the abyss facing Germany.

On the same day, Von Papen received news that his son, serving in the German Army, had been wounded during an air raid in Rennes, and he was in hospital in Paris. He asked Hitler's permission to visit him before returning to Ankara, which was granted. By June he was back in Turkey.[13]

★★★

Sir Hughe Knatchbull-Hugessen was pleased with the new air of co-operation in Ankara: 'In proportion, as Turkey took action against Germany our relations mended.'[14] On 20 April the Turkish government cut the chrome supplies to Germany; in June 'camouflaged German warships' were forbidden the use of the straights; and on 2 August, Turkey broke off relations with Germany.[15]

It does seem that Sir Hughe escaped any serious reprimand at the time for the leak and was later moved to the embassy in Brussels to become ambassador there. However, the security services would later get the 'Foreign Office thoroughly rattled as they should be about the security of Embassies and Legations abroad'.[16] Bazna says he saw Sir Hughe leave the embassy in Ankara in his car to take up the post in Brussels: 'He sat erect against the cushions. I raised my hat, but he did not see me.'[17]

In the few months after Cicero disappeared, Bazna did not leave Ankara but 'rented a smart flat in the Maltere quarter'. There he took up the life of a 'wealthy idler'. He enjoyed Esra's favours, for she was an ideal mistress and 'more like a slave than a girl-friend'. But like the other women he had met, he began to tire of her. He felt it was because she knew him as a *'kavass'* (servant), which was 'something I wanted to forget'. He decided to pay for her university education and send her away. 'She did not weep or make a scene' as Mara had; Esra was Muslim and just embraced the 'inevitable'.

He took up with a Greek songstress called Aika. She had a good figure, though she was not much of a singer, but 'she kept to the rules of the game'. With her blonde hair and long legs she reminded him of 'Cornelia Kapp, who I blamed for having brought Cicero's career to a premature end'.[18]

# 19

# THE LONGEST DAY

In the accounts by Moyzisch and Bazna, both agree that the documents revealing the codename Operation Overlord came from the Allied conference at Tehran in December 1943.[1]

The invasion came as no surprise, as both sides had been preparing for the event for years. From June 1940, when France fell and the British withdrew from Europe, preparations began immediately for their eventual return. Only days after the Dunkirk evacuation, British forces conducted a small raid on the German-occupied coast. This was the beginning of several 'Commando' raids to harass the Germans and compel them to stretch their forces in Europe. The biggest of these raids was the spectacular destruction of the dock at St Nazaire, and the bigger, but ultimately disastrous, landing at Dieppe in 1942.

Rarely, if ever, had an operation been in preparation for so long as the Normandy Landings. From 1942 American troops and vast amounts of supplies were transferred to Britain in what was known as Operation Bolero, the preliminary build up to the cross-Channel attack. However, the North African landings, and then those in Sicily and mainland Italy, siphoned off this strength. The Americans had hoped to launch the invasion in 1943, but the situation in the Mediterranean gained momentum at the expense of Bolero, although the experience there would prove invaluable. The Allies agreed to launch Operation Overlord in the spring of 1944.

In the long story of the build up to D-Day, one point is often overlooked, or given scant coverage, as so much has been written from the Allied point of view. That point was that, in 1941, Adolf Hitler, with his famous intuition, in a directive called 'Construction of Coastal Defences' expected the Allies to attempt landings on 'the protruding points of Normandy and Brittany' where good harbours 'would make ideal beachheads'. This was against the advice of his generals, who expected the landings further north in the Pas de Calais area.[2]

It is unclear what happened to change the Führer's mind in barely two years. In March 1942 he appointed Field Marshal Gerd Von Rundstedt, a dependable soldier, if not the most imaginative, as commander in the west, responsible for the defence of France, Belgium and Holland.

The St Nazaire raid shocked Hitler, but he was heartened by the Dieppe debacle, where the Allies got a bloody nose. He considered Dieppe to be an invasion attempt, even when it was revealed the Canadian troops had orders to return to Britain.

In the third year of the war, the Allies launched Operation Jubilee, the largest cross-Channel foray up to that time. It was an Anglo-Canadian raid to seize Dieppe, to destroy targets, take prisoners and then to re-embark. From the deck of HMS *Fernie*, Ian Fleming watched as his 30 Assault Unit Royal Marines was in action. Later he wrote in a NID report: 'It was difficult to add up the pros and cons of the bloody gallant affair.' Nearly half of the 5,000 Canadian soldiers who set off for Dieppe did not return.[3]

In August 1942 Hitler ordered widespread defences to be constructed, including concrete strongpoints to form a belt of interlocking fire. By the end of September he had outlined his plan: the Atlantic Wall was to consist of 15,000 strongpoints, guarded by 300,000 troops. He wanted the invasion, when it came, to be stopped on the beaches.[4]

In November 1943, Von Rundstedt wrote in his directive 'Preparations for the Struggle' about the Allied plans that: 'Where he will come we do not know; neither do we know when he will come.' At that time the field marshal was not so interested in concrete forts, but more in the 'quality of his combat troops'. He felt the length of the coastline meant the Allies must get ashore somewhere, unless intelligence was improved to give them the when and where. Chief of Staff General Alfred Jodl listed six different places where they might land.[5]

Yet, shortly after this, Cicero had obtained papers from the Tehran Conference that revealed the codename 'Operation Overlord'. From this, Moyzisch worked out the original date for the landings as mid-May 1944.[6] This was, indeed, the original date, but it was later changed to June in the hope of marginally better weather conditions in the English Channel.

Some sources hold that Cicero was a double agent; a British plant as part of 'Operation Bodyguard', the broad deception plan for D-Day which began in 1943 and was presented at the Tehran Conference.

As Churchill aptly remarked, 'Truth is so precious that she should be attended by a bodyguard of lies.'[7]

Cicero began operating before the Tehran Conference, but he could have been turned by the British by that point. This has been put forward by some after Allen Dulles' remark in Switzerland that 'the British were playing some sort of game with Cicero'.[8] Cave Brown also claimed that Menzies, wartime head of MI6, told him in an interview that: 'Of course Cicero was under our control.'[9] He also points to the fact that Bazna was able to 'walk away from the British Embassy a free man'. Similarly, the 'psychological and political warfare aspects' of the documents were most important. The Germans had little real hope of the Grand Alliance breaking up and the country was doomed due to being shackled to the Nazi corpse.[10] However, this also had another effect, as it was mostly high-ranking Nazis that read it and they were now more determined to fight on to the bitter end.

In Maclean's *Take Nine Spies*, a footnote to the Cicero case indicates that H.R. Trevor-Roper, the historian, had concluded that, in the end, Cicero had been used by the British 'to deceive instead of to inform'.[11]

Did the Cicero documents affect German military decisions? Yes they did, but in the main they drew the wrong conclusions or did nothing. Most obvious was in keeping significant numbers of troops in the Balkans, when it was clear the Allies could not undertake two large operations at the same time. The failure of the British in the Aegean while the Italian campaign was in its early stages demonstrated this weakness. In this the Allies were merely lucky, for it was not part of any overall deception campaign, and, as the MI6 investigation into Cicero concludes, 'the potential danger was enormous'.[12]

Had Cicero been part of an overall British deception plan? If so, it would seem to have been an elaborate ploy to send MI6 to investigate the leakage, and the full story did not emerge until after the war. It is also unlikely that Bazna would have been able to curb his enthusiasm about being a double agent: 'His ego could not have resisted such an assertion had it been true.'[13]

Why then did Menzies tell Cave Brown that MI6 controlled Cicero? Firstly, Brown's book was published some time after Menzies' death in 1968. During the war Menzies was in control of SIS and the GC & CS at Bletchley Park, Buckinghamshire, also known as Station X. He basked in the reflected glory within the circles of those who knew about the precious 'Ultra' signals, and was knighted in 1943. With the link strong between the SIS and GC & CS, he was able to fend off proposals for a unified British Secret Service, and any attempts by the armed services departments to take over.

Thus the service was well prepared for the Cold War. He was chief until 1951, and was regarded by his admirers as an intelligence officer 'of the old school'.[14] Kim Philby's defection to the Soviet Union in 1963, and the revelation he had been a Soviet double agent for years, tarnished Menzies' reputation. Philby had been part of the 'Cambridge Five' spy ring, which included Donald Maclean, Guy Burgess and Antony Blunt, while the fifth man has never been confirmed.[15]

Menzies was probably irked by remarks Philby made about him, such as 'I look back on him with both affection and respect', which was surely a veiled gibe at his old chief.[16] It may be that Menzies' claim about Cicero was the action of an embittered man, and possibly he was aiming to take the credit in order to restore his prestige.

Many double agents were used by MI6 in Operation Fortitude, which was built on two main supports almost from scratch: 'strategic deception and the Double Cross system'.[17]

However, it is a mistake to conclude that intelligence decided the outcome of the war, it did not. Germany's attack on the Soviet Union and her declaration of war on the United States after the Japanese surprise attack on the Pacific Fleet at Pearl Harbor in December 1941 sealed her fate. The much greater resources of the Allies made ultimate victory for the Axis impossible. Yet there is equally no doubt that superior Allied intelligence work shortened the conflict and saved millions of lives. Good intelligence made several Allied victories possible. For example, Ultra decrypts helped Admiral Andrew Cunningham's British Mediterranean Fleet defeat the Italian fleet at Matapan in March 1941.[18] Similarly, without Ultra, used to intercept German supply convoys, Erwin Rommel's *Afrika Korps* might well have reached Cairo in 1942. But in the battle for Crete, Ultra could not make up for the lack of air cover, anti-aircraft guns, transport or poor communications on the ground.

Perhaps the most decisive use of intelligence tipped the balance in the Battle of the Atlantic, the largest and most complex naval campaign in history. It reached its height in 1943, and more than anything it was probably Ultra that made the difference against the German U-boats. Victory in the North Atlantic, the most serious challenge Britain faced, allowed the immense build up of forces and equipment that were being readied in Britain for D-Day.

For the landings in June 1944, the Allies required command of the sea and air. But on land the seven Allied divisions would potentially face fifty-nine German divisions in France alone. For the Allies to succeed, they had to convince the Germans the attack would come in the Pas de Calais. The Double Cross system was to be deployed to do this, which in turn depended on Ultra decrypts showing whether the Germans had taken the bait. By 1 June, five days before the landings on the five Normandy beaches, German intelligence believed there were almost ninety Allied Divisions in Britain, as opposed to the real total of forty-seven.[19]

At the start of the Second World War the British Double Cross, or XX, system started as an anti-espionage method run by MI5. From July 1940 the *Abwehr* launched a large-scale espionage campaign against Britain; however, they were a pretty poorly trained bunch and, with the help of the Ultra decrypts, MI5 had no trouble picking up the spies. John C. Masterman, who later controlled the XX Committee, said that, by 1941, MI5 'actively ran and controlled the German espionage system in Britain'. Of twenty-five German agents sent to Britain between September and November 1940, all but one were caught, five were executed, fifteen imprisoned and four became double agents; the lone evader later shot himself.[20]

When either *Abwehr* or SD agents were caught, they were taken to Camp 020, Latchmere House, Richmond, where they would be interrogated by Captain (later Colonel) Robin Stephens and his staff. Known behind his back as 'Tin Eye' for his ever-present monocle, Stephens was a fierce Indian Army veteran. From July 1940 spies were brought to Camp 020 and, although Stephens strictly forbade violence, he did use relentless interrogation techniques. Then, those thought suitable to become double agents fell under the control of Thomas Argyll Robertson, called 'Tar' from his initials, who was a brilliant MI5 man.[21]

The system was also used outside Britain. In particular, agents were run in Spain and Portugal, and some had direct contact with the Germans. Perhaps the most famous agent of the Double Cross system was codenamed 'Garbo' by the British and 'Arabel' by the Germans. Juan Pujol Garcia was from the Catalan region of Spain and, during the Spanish Civil War, developed a loathing for the Fascists and Communists. During the early part of the Second World War, he contacted both the

British and American intelligence agencies with an offer to work for them, but was initially rejected. Undeterred, he created a pro-Nazi identity and became a German agent. He was instructed to travel to Britain and recruit agents, and he began to invent fictional agents and send in reports based on tourist guides of Britain. After an approach to the US Navy attaché in Lisbon, Lieutenant Patrick Demorest called in his British counterparts. At last Garbo was taken seriously and, in a few months, was in England. After a thorough MI5 debriefing to make sure he was genuine, finally the British accepted Garbo. Like Cicero, he was termed a 'walk-in' and was unique among double agents, having set out to be so.

★★★

However, it was what was in Adolf Hitler's mind above all that mattered. By 1944 that mind was confused and was already being affected by the onset of Parkinson's disease, combined with his hysterical disposition.

In November 1943 Hitler ordered that the coastline defences should be further strengthened with concrete emplacements and beach obstacles, and even heavy guns from idle warships were mounted in batteries. He also saw the need for strong mobile reserves, for if the Allies broke through the Atlantic Wall, then they should be strongly counter-attacked. To do this, Hitler had previously ordered two crack Panzer divisions from the Soviet Union to the Atlantic Wall, the 'Adolf Hitler' and '*Grossdeutschland*', even when they were badly needed on the Eastern Front.[22]

To ensure the Atlantic Wall was in good hands, he transferred Erwin Rommel and his Army Group B Headquarters from Lake Garda in Italy to France, and Rommel was subordinated to Rundstedt. The ever-energetic Rommel certainly improved the defences; he felt the invasion should be stopped on the beaches and destroyed within forty-eight hours. On one inspection tour of the Atlantic Wall he told his officers:

> Believe me, gentlemen, the twenty-four hours of the invasion will be decisive. For the Allies, but also for the Germans, it will be the long-est day.[23]

1 Elyesa Bazna, dressed for a singing recital at about the time he began his exploits as Agent Cicero.

2 Elyesa Bazna in the 1960s.

3  L.C. Moyzisch, the SD man who was Cicero's link to the Germans throughout his period as a spy.

4 The German Embassy in Ankara in the 1960s.

5 The British Embassy in Ankara in the 1960s.

6 Franz Von Papen, German ambassador to Turkey 1939–44.

7 Sir Hughe Knatchbull-Hugessen, British ambassador to Turkey (left), in conversation with the Turkish president, Ismet Inonu. (Getty Images)

Constantinople.
Dec. 12. 09.

H.K.H.

8  Drawing of the Golden Horn, Istanbul. (Hughe Knatchbull-Hugessen, 1909)

9 Opel Admiral. This type of car was used for the meetings between Moyzisch and Cicero. (Opel Centre, Berlin)

10 Reich Foreign Minister Joachim Von Ribbentrop in the uniform of an *SS-Standartenführer.* (*Bundesarchiv*)

11  Ernst Kaltenbrunner, head of the SD and RSHA.

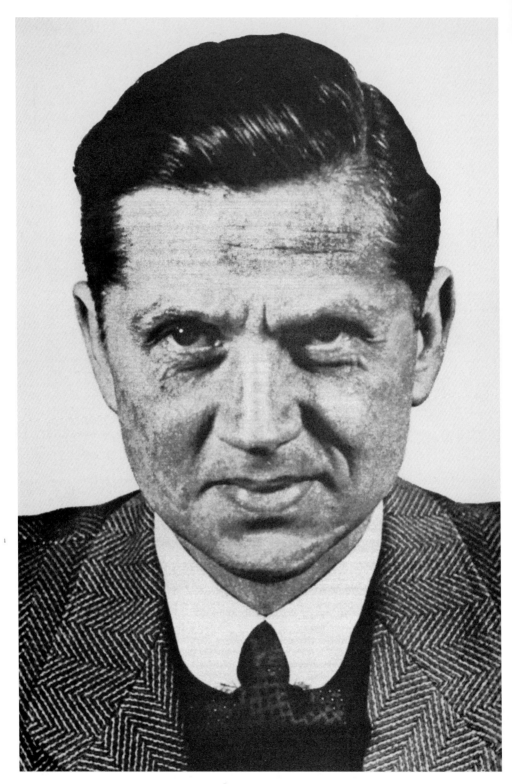

12 Walther Schellenberg, enthusiastic supporter of the Cicero documents, friend of Moyzisch, and later head of the SD. (*Bundesarchiv*)

13  First wartime meeting of Churchill and Roosevelt on board the battleship HMS *Prince of Wales*, 1941. (USN Historical Centre)

14  Atlantic Conference, 1941, on board HMS *Prince of Wales*. Being well aware of Roosevelt's disability, Churchill sat with the president during the Sunday service. (USN Historical Centre)

15 Meeting of the 'Big Three' – Stalin, Roosevelt and Churchill – at the Tehran Conference, November–December 1943. (US National Archives)

16 Roosevelt, Churchill and Inonu at the second Cairo Conference, 4–6 December 1943. (US Library of Congress)

17 Allan Dulles, OSS officer in Switzerland who first came across Cicero via the Fritz Kolbe papers, which he supplied to the British. Later director of the CIA.

18 Von Papen and Hitler in conversation at Berchtesgaden, probably early in the war.

19 US troops landing on D-Day, 6 June 1944. Had the Germans used the Cicero documents wisely, there could have been many more German troops available to counter the invasion. (US National Archives)

# A war spy in the British Embassy

## Astonishing story of an ambassador's valet

IN a Belgian newspaper an astonishing story is being published.

It tells how in 1943 the Germans obtained vitally important Allied war secrets by paying £300,000 in sterling to the valet of the British Ambassador to Turkey, Sir Hughe Knatchbull-Hugessen.

In this way, it is said, they 'arned of the Moscow and 'blanca conference deci- 'ms, details of the bomber o'ensives, and plans for the '' invasion of Europe. T'' also obtained the key to the British diplomatic code.

### An offer

THE disclosure is made by the German official who claims to have handled the transaction.

His name is [L. C. Moyzisch]. He was known to the British as head of the German spy system in Ankara during the war.

His story, told in the florid style of spy-thriller fiction, amounts in brief to this.

On October 26, 1943, Moyzisch was approached in his office at the German Embassy, Ankara, by a "peculiar individual," who claimed that he had "an exceptional offer to make the Germans."

### Nervous look

'oyzisch describes him as "a about 50, with a large fore-'head, sparse black hair, sombre eyes, with a nervous look."

The man warned Moyzisch that the slightest indiscretion would cost them both their lives. He then said that he could

British Embassy, and said that when brushing the ambassador's clothes at night he was able to acquire the keys of the safe.

His task was made easier, claimed Cicero, because the ambassador was in the habit of taking sleeping tablets.

Moyzisch calls (Cornelie) She learned the nature of Moyzisch's relations with Cicero, and a few days later disappeared without trace.

At this point Moyzisch's story becomes a full-blooded spy thriller.

THE BRITISH EMBASSY at Ankara in 1943

P.F. 66.383

### Sir Hughe Knatchbull-Hugessen

Hughe Knatchbull-Hugessen at his home in Kent.

His reply was frank.

"The backbone of the story is certainly true. There is a basis of truth in it, but it has been subjected to a great deal of imaginative treatment.

"There are incidents in it—such as my taking sleeping tablets—which are quite untrue.

"The whole business, as far as intense activity was concerned, took place in a period of about six weeks.

"Within a few days of discovering it we were able to stop what was going on.

Discharged

20 *Sunday Express* headline, January 1950, breaking the story of the Cicero Affair. (Public Records Office)

21 The French actress Danielle Darrieux, who played Countess Anna Staviska in the film *Five Fingers*. Anna was a purely fictional character invented for the film.

22  James Mason as Cicero and Oscar Karlweis as Moyzisch in the film *Five Fingers.*

23 James Mason in his most famous role as Erwin Rommel in *The Desert Fox*.

The two German commanders differed in their approach: Rommel wanted every soldier in the west dug in on the shoreline, while Rundstedt was trying to retain a large mobile reserve because he felt the Allies would get through the Atlantic Wall somewhere. Rommel's view was based on the power of the Allied air forces, which would make movement of reserves extremely difficult, and Allied naval guns would so cover the beach areas as to make regaining them impossible.[24]

Von Papen witnessed the power of the Allied air forces when he visited his wounded son in hospital near Paris:

> I was shocked to see the destruction caused by Allied air attacks in the large towns along this route. It was only just possible to keep the trains circulating, and in France the Allied air forces had for weeks been bombing bridges, cuttings and marshalling yards.

After seeing his son, Von Papen went to visit Rundstedt at his headquarters; he found the field marshal 'desperate', as 'the systematic destruction of the railway network was making the rapid movement of reserves impossible'. He confided to Von Papen that, in his opinion, 'a landing on a major scale could not be contested'.[25]

Hitler never gave clear overall direction to either of his commanders, so neither theory of defence gained priority. He still thought a landing in Normandy most likely, but he strongly believed a second landing would take place in the narrower part of the Channel. It was the shortest route into Germany and very close to the V weapons deployed behind this area; Hitler believed that these weapons could still win the war for Germany. Operation Fortitude, the great British deception plan using the Double Cross agents, was rather taken at face value by the High Command. For Hitler, too, the information it supplied fitted the theory in his mind. Thus, the German Fifteenth Army, with fifteen divisions, were positioned north of the Seine, and held there on Hitler's orders.[26]

Hitler had scored an own goal by virtually disbanding the *Abwehr* in February after the Vermehren Affair in Istanbul, where Menzies and MI6 had managed 'to throw a spanner in the German works'. While the Vermehrens went over to the British, four other German agents were lured away by the OSS, led by their Istanbul chief, Lanning Macfarland.[27]

However, not all those within British intelligence were so happy at the demise of the *Abwehr*.

The Double Cross team were horrified, as 'The *Abwehr* officers were the devils they knew'. Masterman recognised the danger that the 'new brooms would sweep away much which we had tried to preserve'.[28] However, it was the likes of Philby and Blunt who represented the great danger to the Double Cross operation. Blunt supplied Moscow with a 'torrential leakage of information' – he sent 1,771 documents to Soviet intelligence – and, if the Germans penetrated the network, then the information would undoubtedly end up in Berlin.[29]

Schellenberg took over the *Abwehr* and incorporated it into the SD, but fortunately for the Allies he only managed to create an inefficient muddle at a crucial time for Germany. The *Abwehr* had not been such a bad organisation: it had managed to sustain surveillance in the United States and Britain to a fairly high degree under difficult conditions. It also obtained reliable information and enabled the German High Command to follow the growing Anglo-American strategic concept of the invasion plan, from its birth in 1942 to the arrival of the Allies in Normandy in 1944.

By the time of D-Day, German intelligence was still in a poor state and, on 4 June, the German High Command were reportedly 'groping completely in the dark'. The *Kriegsmarine* (German Navy) commander in France, Admiral Theodor Krancke, said: 'It's doubtful whether the enemy has yet assembled his invasion fleet in the required strength.' The next day, Rundstedt said: 'As yet there is no immediate prospect of invasion.'[30]

Admiral Krancke cancelled naval patrols in the Channel for the night of 5 June, no doubt waiting for the storm that had postponed Operation Neptune by twenty-four hours to pass. Rommel went home on the same day to spend a night with his family and celebrate his wife's birthday in Heerlinden; he planned to see Hitler at Berchtesgaden the next day to argue his case for reinforcing the troops in Normandy. Friedrich Dollmann, commander of Seventh Army, was in Rennes at a map exercise, and he had even reduced the alert state of his troops because of the bad weather, while Sepp Dietrich, commander of 1st SS Panzer Corps, was in Brussels. Therefore, as a consequence of the lack of reliable intelligence, of the five principal commanders in the west, three were not at their headquarters when the invasion began.[31]

General Walter Warlimont, Jodl's deputy, wrote in his memoirs:

… the day before the invasion, German Supreme Headquarters had not the slightest idea that the decisive event of the war was upon them.

For twenty-four hours more than five thousand ships had been on the move across the Channel toward the coast of Normandy but there had been no reconnaissance to spot them.

Yet from another source, the *Abwehr*, it appears there were warnings of impending invasion. Warlimont wrote:

> ... that as early as January 1944, Admiral Canaris had discovered the text of a two-part radio message to be transmitted from England shortly before the invasion as a standby signal to the French Resistance ...
>
> On the afternoon of 5 June, the Intelligence Service informed Jodl that during the night of 4 June the second of these two sentences had been heard by the Security Section of 15th Army. But no action was taken.

Nobody at the time seems to have paid the slightest attention to these reports. The first had come to the *Abwehr* in October 1943, the second to the RSHA on 2 June 1944, and the third on 4 June to the RSHA. But with no Canaris, now virtually under open arrest, and the *Abwehr* in tatters, no one realised the importance of this information, nor did it fit their preconceptions.

This leakage was the result of the collapse of SOE/resistance cells in France. In July 1943 Menzies had learnt that resistance networks in France 'might be a danger to the security of Overlord'. The Paris network was one of the biggest; led by Major Francis Suttill and code-named 'Prosper', it had the task of preparing the French Resistance for the invasion.[32] The group was compromised in June 1943; Suttill was arrested and tortured, but although he was aware of the 'alert' signal, it is unlikely that he revealed this. He was later executed by firing squad at Sachsenhausen concentration camp. Quite how many people where taken on the collapse of Prosper is hard to estimate, but figures of between 400 and 1,500 have been quoted, and, no doubt, one of Prosper's deputies did reveal the 'alert'. Hitler gave the order to dismantle Prosper in the belief that this would so disrupt the Allies that they would abandon any invasion attempt in 1943. This also gave the German High Command the opportunity to switch divisions from France to the other fighting fronts, replacing them with exhausted units and allowing for rest and new equipment.

The *Abwehr* had also penetrated other groups in France and Holland, but the disruption of the *Abwehr* relegated much of its work and good material to gather dust in files.

At 1 a.m. on 6 June, 'Garbo' radioed his *Abwehr* controller, Karl Erich Kuhlenthal, who had not been lost in the reshuffle, that the Allied forces had embarked for Normandy. The message was too late to assist the defenders, but, as it was designed to do, the information enhanced his reputation with the Germans. Then, on 9 June, he sent another message requesting it be sent on to the High Command urgently:

> The present operation though a large scale assault is diversionary in character.

This reinforced Hitler's belief there would be another landing in the Pas de Calais, and the message arrived in time for Hitler to cancel the movement of 1st SS Panzer and 116th Panzer Divisions to Normandy.

He awarded 'Radio Arabel' (Garbo) the Iron Cross 2nd class, while Cicero was paid with counterfeit money. This incident clearly demonstrates 'the ascendancy of the British intelligence community over its German opponent'.[33]

At a military situation conference in December 1943, Hitler commented about the Cicero documents that: 'I have mostly studied through these documents. There is absolutely no doubt that the attack in the west is coming in the spring.'[34] He outlined possible deceptions the Allies might try: in Norway, the Bordeaux area in France, and the Balkans. He also pointed out telegram No. 1751 from the British Foreign Office to the Ankara Embassy. An 'immediate' signal bearing the highest security rating, 'Most Secret', and the code word 'Bigot' added gave restricted access to only a few people. In it was the text of a message from the British chiefs of staff to General Eisenhower, indicating their aim 'to get Turkey into the war' and to 'maintain a threat to the Germans until Overlord is launched'. Certainly 'threat' here meant a deception or scare tactic. Yet one's conclusion must be that Hitler never really believed the Cicero documents because, by and large, they told him what he did not want to hear.

He ignored the good information about the Balkans and committed twenty-five German divisions there, including two Panzer divisions. They were held there away from the main battles, facing only small-scale raids by bands of partisans and British Commandos.

In a report, MI6 identified this as the crucial point: '... through the leakage, the Germans became aware that there was no genuine threat of an Allied move in the Balkans'. Jodl's diary also confirmed this information had reached the German High Command. In conclusion, the report states: '... perhaps Cicero earned all the money the Germans paid him'.[35]

# 20

# WAR'S END

As soon as Von Papen returned to Ankara, the Allies landed in Normandy. Once it became apparent the Germans could not dislodge the Allied armies and drive them into the sea, the Turkish government severed diplomatic relations with Germany on 2 August. Von Papen felt this was 'a sorry end to my mission'.[1] Ribbentrop sent orders for him to return to Germany, but it was a bad time to go home as the country was in a frenzy after the July attempt on Hitler's life.[2]

The 20 July 1944 had dawned hot and sultry, when Count Claus Schenk Von Stauffenberg flew to meet Hitler at a military conference at the Wolf's Lair headquarters in East Prussia. In the conference room he left behind a briefcase containing two small bombs, placed under the table. He was then called away by a bogus telephone call. Somehow the briefcase was moved further away from Hitler. At 12.42 p.m. it exploded with a deafening roar; four men were killed, but Hitler survived, stumbling from the building, bruised and bloodied with burst eardrums.[3]

Von Papen left Turkey on 5 August by train. It passed through Belgrade after a heavy air raid: 'But when we got to Budapest the beautiful city on the Danube lay unharmed in the August sunlight'. However, towards the end of the war the city would become a devastated battleground and suffer heavy loss of life. As the train approached the German frontier he became apprehensive, expecting to be met by the Gestapo and arrested. He travelled with his granddaughter; he gave her a message for his wife who was already at home in Germany in case he did not return. At the very least he felt his name was on the list for questioning.

However, he successfully crossed the border with no problems, and continued on the train to Berlin. He felt arrest might be waiting for him there, but, instead of the Gestapo, he was met by people from the Foreign Ministry, who told him he 'had no reason to fear arrest, although tension in the capital was at breaking point'. He was also told to report to the Wolf's Lair the next day.[4]

Moyzisch managed to avoid going home; he became engrossed in helping organise the evacuation of the large German community once diplomatic relations were severed with Turkey. There were 2,000 people in total and they had to go by the end of August or risk internment. Three trains were scheduled for the evacuation. He put himself and his family down for the last train, with no real wish to go home where an unknown fate awaited him. But the last train never left Ankara, for Red Army troops had cut the railway line between Sofia and Belgrade.

Moyzisch was interned with his family and a few other members of the embassy, although this amounted to staying in the embassy building: 'the only change being that we were surrounded by a few strands of barbed wire and Turkish sentries walked up and down outside'.[5]

\*\*\*

Bazna dabbled in the second-hand car trade in Ankara as the war wound down, but he soon became bored. He moved in with Aika, his tall and beautiful mistress, who he felt made 'an excellent impression' on Istanbul. They travelled a lot, before Bazna decided he would build a hotel in Bursa on 'Swiss lines'. He found a building contractor in Istanbul who was willing to partner him and they founded the firm of Bazna and Oztemel:

Nobody asked where I came from, or where my money came from, or how I used to earn my living.[6]

The new firm obtained government contracts to build a post office in Istanbul and a school in Bursa. Bazna also decided to buy the Celik Hotel in Bursa, an 'old-fashioned establishment', which he would rebuild and call the 'Celik Palace'. However, his partner found it too risky and they eventually parted company. A new man joined him, Niyazi Acar, and they formed Bazna and Acar.

It was while he was discussing plans for the 'Celik Palace' with architects that a telephone call came to bring his world crashing down around him. On the other end of the line, his partner, Acar, told him in an 'excited' voice that he had been visited by the police and the firm's assets had been seized. Some of the payments Bazna made had been with forged British banknotes. Bazna collapsed, and the bewildered architects immediately called Aika:

> When the delirium subsided I was completely calm, listless, and apathetic. Aika realised more clearly than I did the meaning of that telephone call. She left me the same evening.[7]

★★★

At Hitler's headquarters Von Papen first met with Ribbentrop, who was 'full of assumed indignation at the "perfidy" of the Turks in breaking off relations, and raging at the "bourgeois traitors" of the July plot'. Later he saw Hitler, who had a heavy screen of security about him. Visitors now had to surrender 'hats, coats, brief cases and anything else they were carrying'.

In the Führer's ante-room he waited until Hitler came in: he was 'ashen pale, one arm in a sling, trembling in every limb. The man was a nervous wreck.' Hitler tried to be upbeat and to minimise what had happened, but talk of 'traitors' made his eyes shine with hatred. He asked Von Papen for his news.

He told him of the last events in Ankara, how the Allies had put 'pressure' on the Turks to break off relations with Germany, emphasising that many Turks had been reluctant to comply. To his surprise Hitler seemed 'satisfied with my account' and he had thought the Turks might throw in their lot with the Allies 'ever since the loss of the Crimea'.

Von Papen says he turned the conversation to the general war situation, and how it was best to employ their 'strategic advantage of interior lines'. Suggesting they should hold the Russians at all costs and try to reach agreement with the Allies, he pointed out the Cicero documents demonstrated they might still rescue 'what was left of Europe' with skilful diplomacy.

Hitler would not listen and his rage returned: 'Livid patches appeared in his white haggard face.' He spoke in short staccato sentences: the war had to be fought to the bitter end; new weapons would tip the balance; they would show the British. 'With such people there can be no compromise.'

Just before Von Papen left, Hitler gave him a small case containing the Knight's Cross of the Military Merit Order. Awarded for his many services to the country, he too had served on the frontline, said Hitler, as the attempt on Von Papen's life demonstrated. They shook hands for the last time.[8]

★★★

In August Sir Hughe Knatchbull-Hugessen left Ankara. Brussels was liberated on 8 September, in scenes of near-delirium, and the new British ambassador arrived seventeen days later. The city was still very much in the frontline and still vulnerable to V1s, while London was then under attack by V2s. Nevertheless, Sir Hughe found: 'Every house in Brussels had its flag and the whole town was decked as for some gala day'. The flags remained out for many months. He also found little 'outward signs of starvation' which he had feared he might find.[9]

He found the embassy on the Rue de Spa in a mess, with furniture piled up in every room. The house had been used as a store by British subjects hurriedly leaving the country in May 1940. It was two months before they could move into the house and he bemoaned the lack of anything 'respectable' in the cellar:

> For a long time our guests at luncheon or dinner were regaled with pike and rabbit washed down with what can only be described as something red or something white.[10]

★★★

For Moyzisch and others interned at the German Embassy in Ankara, they could do nothing but wait for a ship to take them home. The ship would most probably be Swedish, as they were one of the few nations that would be given free passage by the Allied navies and the German passengers would have diplomatic immunity.

'Again I was lucky,' says Moyzisch, as it wasn't until the end of April 1945 that a ship was available, the *Drottningholm*, and, by then, Hitler was dead and the war in Europe was close to an end.[11]

The Moyzisch family joined the ship at Istanbul. By the time they reached Gibraltar the war was over. However, as a result, Moyzisch had lost his diplomatic immunity and he was interned by the British, first in England at Camp 020 and later in the British Zone in Germany.[12]

★★★

Von Papen was only too glad to get back to his home in Wallerfangen on the Franco-German border, which he reached in September 1944, but he was met in this quiet backwater by the retreating German armies making for the Rhine:

> There seemed to be no order and no plan, only the panic-stricken rush of those who were trying to save their skins.[13]

With US troops having reached the Moselle River, and German cities being reduced to rubble by Allied bombers, Von Papen contacted the Foreign Ministry with an offer to go to Madrid. There he would contact the Western Allies with a plan for them to occupy Germany while German forces held on in the east. A reply came back from Ribbentrop, in no uncertain terms, that anyone engaging in 'such discussions would be shot as a defeatist'. He was ordered to move deeper into Germany with his family. They took only 'bare necessities' and all the valuables in the house were locked away in the cellars. He moved to the house of a friend near Koblenz: 'We had become refugees like so many of our countrymen.' Later he learned the US Army removed everything from the Wallerfangen house and burned it to the ground.[14]

On 23 February 1945 Turkey declared war on Germany, but by then Von Papen had other worries. In March the Allies had reached the Rhine, and Von Papen and his family were on the move again. He was being constantly watched and any mail he received was first diverted by the post office and read by the Gestapo. He and his family made their way to his married daughter's home at Stockhausen, Westphalia, but the war soon arrived there too. He moved from the main house with his daughter and children to a small lodge in the woods 'as the battle crept ever nearer'. On 9 April his son-in-law was taken as a prisoner of war.

The next day an American infantry platoon arrived at the lodge and 'the sergeant challenged my identity'. Von Papen was immediately arrested, despite protesting that he had no military command and was 'over sixty-five years old'. It was of no use, though, as the Americans had their orders to take him in for questioning:

> We invited him to sit down while I finished a plate of stew with the children; then I packed a few things into a rucksack and went off with him in his jeep.[15]

# 21

# TRIAL AND REVELATION

In complete ignorance that his money was worthless, Bazna was quick to spread it about before it was identified as counterfeit. All this took place within Turkey, and he claimed to have given Mara money for her dowry, funded Esra through university, and sent money to his ex-wife and her four children.[1] Once he was found to be the source of the fake money, he had an on-going battle with the police, courts and creditors. He told the Turkish police his story and how he had been duped by the Germans:

> The Courts finally gave up trying to stamp me as a criminal. But they insisted on my repaying the debts that I had contracted by unknowingly paying bills with forged money.

He then met a woman named Duriet, who became his wife and knew he was 'poor'. He resided with her in a modest house at Zulali Cesme Sokak, Istanbul. He had four more children with Duriet, and began seeing his other four children from his previous marriage from time to time. His income came from giving singing lessons, running a small import-export business, and he tried the used car trade again, but what profit he made went to pay his creditors.[2]

★★★

Moyzisch went through a lengthy interrogation at Camp 020 and, in July 1945, in a monthly summary, it was observed that on his first arrival he had denied 'all acquaintance with espionage and agents'. However, he had 'been broken to the extent that he admits to a number of clandestine sources … and to a limited knowledge of the G.I.S [German

Intelligence Service] machine in Turkey'. They managed to go further and to induce him to reveal more about the 'penetration' of the British Embassy in Ankara.[3]

Yet his interrogators still suspected him of holding out. A letter from Major C. O'Brien of Camp 020 to Colonel H.L.A. Hart of MI5 indicates that 'Moyzisch is misleading the interrogators'. And that they knew from Vermehren that Moyzisch:

> … had a source in the Turkish Foreign Ministry from whom he obtained copies of detailed reports on Allied war materials sent to Turkey. This information he passed personally to Von Papen. This is another point on which Moyzisch might well be pressed.[4]

It is likely that these details came to German attention not from a Turkish source but from the Cicero documents.

Schellenberg was also held at Camp 020, and, while he was being driven by an 'English Officer' from Richmond to a special Anglo-American commission on codes, he was asked what he thought of Moyzisch. He says he just 'shrugged his shoulders', not wanting to answer. The officer continued quizzing him about Moyzisch, but Schellenberg remained non-committal. The officer then told him Moyzisch had commented that he was 'really Jewish, and that you forced him to join the SS and work for you at pistol point'.[5]

Moyzisch was released in October and sent home to Vienna. There he joined his wife and children, who had spent some time in Sweden while they were apart. He was later called to the Nuremberg Trials to give evidence, although no charge was ever made against him.[6]

After his arrest, Von Papen was taken to Wiesbaden army headquarters. There he learnt of the death of President Roosevelt, which, he thought, 'seemed a disaster'. He was also told of the terrible conditions found in the concentration camps.[7] After several months, and moves, he found himself in prison at Nuremberg, where he was confined to cell No. 47. He made a calendar on the wall of his cell to mark the passage of time.

A detailed interrogation began in September, which broadly covered his political career, and in October he received a copy of the indictment against him. The case was set for 20 November 1945 and he 'observed with a feeling of relief that there were no charges against me under the heading of war crimes or crimes against humanity'. Instead, he was charged with 'having conspired to wage war'. Yet he was confident he would be able to prove his innocence, and wrote to his wife he was sure he would soon be released. However, he had not been aware that he would figure in a protracted mass trial of 'war criminals'.[8]

For Von Papen, prison was something akin to solitary confinement. The defence lawyers complained to the court several times about prison conditions, but they were told these security precautions were in place to prevent attempts at suicide. Nevertheless, several prisoners succeeded in committing suicide, most notably Hermann Goering. Von Papen says that, on two occasions, his American guards offered him the means to kill himself 'to escape certain hanging'.

On trial days the defendants 'were each given a decent suit every morning in which to appear before the Court, together with ties and shoelaces,' which were taken away again at the end of the day. They sat together frequently for nearly a year.[9]

It was in June 1946 that Von Papen's examination began. Going through his part in Hitler's rise to power, he spoke in the witness box in his defence for three days. He was cross-examined by Sir David Maxwell Fyfe, who reasoned that Von Papen had helped bring Hitler to power with full knowledge of the true nature of the Nazis.

On 30 September the court assembled to hear the verdict; the room was packed with the world's press. Von Papen waited and 'was prepared for the worst', as he felt it was purely a 'political trial'. The reading of the verdict took the whole of that day and part of the next.

Lord Justice Lawrence read the individual verdicts, starting with Goering. Von Papen was fifth from the end and, when his turn came, he was acquitted and released. He had, the verdict said, committed a number of 'political immoralities', but these actions were not punishable. However, that was not the end of Von Papen's ordeal. Upon his release, the Bavarian police placed him under surveillance and he was told not to leave Nuremberg. In poor health, suffering from a heart condition, he found refuge in the hospital of St Theresa, having been refused treatment at the city hospital.

He then faced trial at the German denazification court, where he was charged with assisting the Nazis and having profited from the regime. He was found guilty and condemned to eight years' hard labour and his property confiscated. Still in ill health, Von Papen went to the hospital at Fuerth labour camp, and then to Regensburg camp, where he was badly beaten by a fellow prisoner who was mentally disturbed and in the wrong prison. In 1949 his case went to appeal and, with some bargaining, his sentence was reduced and he was released.[10]

Like Moyzisch, Schellenberg appeared as a witness at the Nuremberg Trials, having returned from Sweden in June 1945. However, he was brought before an American military tribunal on the Wilhelmstrasse Case and charged with crimes against humanity, along with twenty other prominent members of the SD, SS and former Reich ministries. The case was known as the 'Subsequent Nuremberg Trials'.

He was acquitted on all but two charges, which were being a member of the SS and being complicit in the execution without trial of some Russian prisoners, but this was mitigated by his efforts to aid some prisoners in concentration camps in the latter stages of the war. He was sentenced to six years' imprisonment, which was one of the lightest sentences imposed by the court. While in prison he had to undergo a serious operation, and in June 1951 he was released as an act of clemency.[11]

Other Nazi leaders who figured prominently in the Cicero story were not so lucky. Ernst Kaltenbrunner, head of the SD, and Joachim Von Ribbentrop, Reich Minister for Foreign Affairs, were both condemned to death at the Nuremberg Trials and hanged in October 1946.

★★★

The first of the main players in the Cicero affair to release his memoirs was Sir Hughe Knatchbull-Hugessen in 1949 as *Diplomat in Peace and War*. Naturally there is nothing in it about Cicero, or even a passing reference to his valet when he was ambassador in Ankara. He would have been well aware of the case from the security services, although the Official Secrets Act, no doubt to his relief, provided a welcome excuse to omit it from his story.

In the introduction to his memoirs, he quotes a Chinese curse: 'May you live in interesting times' and comments 'our generation had certainly witnessed the curse's fulfilment'.[12] In 1947 he had retired from his post of ambassador to Belgium and envoy to Luxembourg.

In 1950 Moyzisch's book was published in Frankfurt as *Der Fall Cicero* by Die Quadriga, and published in the USA by Coward-McCain, with a postscript by Von Papen, at the same time. The ensuing storm engulfed all concerned.

It first came to light in a Belgian newspaper as *L'Affaire Ciceron*, which was featured by the *Sunday Express* in January in full broadsheet, with a smiling Sir Hughe and a picture of the British Embassy in Ankara.[13] Sir Hughe was surprised by the publicity, but he did admit to John Prebble, in the *Sunday Express* article, that 'The back bone of the story was certainly true', though 'it had been subjected to a great deal of imaginative treatment'. It was 'quite untrue' that he took sleeping pills, and, of Bazna, he thought: 'After this business he was discharged or left.' It was quite apparent that he did not know.[14]

In October the case came before Parliament in London, where Foreign Secretary Ernest Bevin sharply rebuked Sir Hughe in front of the house for not following the rules of security for the custody of documents. He largely maintained his silence on the affair, but in private he was apt to dismiss its significance.[15]

In secret, Dick White of MI5 wrote in his report that 'Moyzisch's book is reasonably authentic'. He requested that a copy of the report should go 'to the Foreign Office'. The CIA also described *Operation Cicero* as 'a competent and factual piece of work'.[16]

Von Papen also publicly endorsed Moyzisch's account in the postscript, saying 'apart from a few details' it was 'perfectly correct'. However, he was well aware that conflict between government departments was cursed with mistrust. Ribbentrop and the Foreign Ministry did not trust Kaltenwbrunner and the RSHA. Anything going into the Foreign Ministry diplomatic bag had to pass before Von Papen and generally Moyzisch used this service. Later Von Papen said he was surprised to learn that Moyzisch did send more sensitive material direct to the RSHA through the SD courier service, bypassing the Foreign Office altogether. It seems odd that Von Papen was surprised, for he was well aware that Moyzisch, like himself, was trying to serve more than one master.

Although Von Papen knew nothing about Cicero's warning of the 'Sofia raid' until *Operation Cicero* was published, he felt that using the raid as a test of the documents without warning the Bulgarians was 'nothing short of criminal'. He went on to indicate how the documents helped him to keep Turkey out of the war, but he would 'have more to say on that subject later'.[17] By 'later', Von Papen was referring to the release of his own memoirs, published in 1952, which contain an entire chapter on the Cicero case.

The release of the feature film *Five Fingers* in 1952, starring James Mason as Cicero, kept the case in the limelight. It was based largely on Moyzisch's book; it was popular and praised by the critics. Darryl F. Zanuck had swiftly obtained the film rights for Twentieth Century Fox, and Michael Wilson wrote the screenplay, for which he was nominated for an academy award. The opening of the film claimed it was a true story, but huge liberties were taken and large parts were no more than fiction. Joseph Mankiewicz directed and Danielle Darrieux supplied the 'love interest', joining Mason in a good cast.[18]

No doubt, after having come across references to Moyzisch's book, Bazna learned about the filming and approached the director, Mankiewicz, expecting a screen role or to be being hired as a consultant. The two men met in a hotel garden chosen by Bazna, while Mankiewicz had photographs taken secretly. He thought the former spy 'the most obvious looking villain I've ever met'. One of the photographs appeared in *Life* magazine in 1952 when the publication reviewed the film, but Bazna was refused any part or payment.

Bazna was still being chased by creditors and directly approached the Germans to ease his financial plight. However, he was turned down by the German Consulate-General of the new Federal Republic of West Germany on the grounds that they had no knowledge of 'Operation Cicero'.[19]

He then approached Albert Jenke, who had returned to Turkey to restart his contracting business. He certainly knew about the case and Bazna had once been his servant, but it counted for little. On his visit, Bazna was asked to wait at the door and 'had to wait a long time'. Then the maid returned and informed him Herr Jenke could not see him. A few days later, Jenke died in a boating accident in the Sea of Marmara when his boat overturned. The newspapers recorded that Jenke, according to the post mortem, 'died of heart failure as a result of shock', so that avenue for potential funds was closed to Bazna.[20]

He even tried singing to earn money; borrowing evening dress, he hired a cinema for a night and printed advertising bills for the concert. Only a few hundred people came, although Bazna says: 'There was great applause after every song'. However, in the audience was one of his creditors and the night's takings were confiscated by a bailiff. So he ended up by owing even more money.[21]

As a last resort, he wrote to the Chancellor of Germany, Dr Konrad Adenauer, saying he had been treated shabbily by the German Reich.

Four months later he got a letter stating that they were unable to take action in his 'claim against German Reich'.[22]

It was shortly after the publication of Moyzisch's account that Bazna started writing his own in a green children's exercise book, and it would be almost a decade before it was published as *I Was Cicero*. He needed help to do so, and he managed to get a journalist, Hans Nogly, interested.

In 1961 the two men met in the Vier Jahreszeiten Hotel in Munich. Nogly started off by 'mistrusting him completely', for he found the 'short, bald, thickset, elderly man' ogling a pretty girl, and the first thing Bazna said to him was: 'What a lot of pretty girls there are in Munich.' His roving eye had not changed in twenty years. He hardly struck Nogly as one of the world's most famous spies, yet his story was still intriguing. During the ensuing conversation, Bazna admitted in his rough written account that he was a 'great hero', but then he had 'a mighty fine opinion of himself'. Nogly asked why he was trying to 'sell his life-story' at this time, to which Bazna replied that he was taking legal action against the West German government for the money the 'Germans cheated me out of when I spied for them'.[23]

To check what seemed to be an improbable claim by this man, Nogly took Bazna to see Moyzisch, then living in Innsbruck. At that meeting, Bazna says they 'smiled coolly' at each other, interested to see how life had treated them: 'We felt no particular sympathy for each other. Our great adventure had rewarded neither.'[24]

In the MI5 report, updated in 1962 to include Bazna's book, it is described as containing 'so much falsehood that, unless independently corroborated, it is worthless as evidence'.[25] This is harsh, given that Bazna's book provides much information on the later background of one of the key players, Cornelia Kapp.

Kapp's post-war fate remained largely unknown until the publication of *I Was Cicero*. On arrival in the USA, she was placed in a North Dakota detention camp, where she says she was given electric 'shock treatment of the kind that is given to the mentally ill'. She was then imprisoned in Washington with 'prostitutes'. At the end of the war, she was living in New Jersey and later moved to Chicago, becoming a 'restaurant hostess', before finally ending up living in California, where she married and had children.[26]

In early 1962, Nogly engaged a journalist, G. Thomas Beyl, to trace Cornelia Kapp through friends in Chicago. He found out she had worked at the Toffinetti's Triangle restaurant, owned by Mr Coutandin, a German who had gone to America at the end of the First World War. While in Chicago she was visited once a week by the FBI. In 1947 she attempted suicide when she learnt of her father's death, who she felt she had betrayed. Beyl located her in San Diego, California, where she was married; her husband worked for the US Navy as a buyer and they lived on a naval base. There he finally interviewed her. He found out she had tried to locate her Cleveland lover, only to find out he was dead.[27]

Cornelia was visited in California by the Coutandin's daughter who found her living on the coast with lively children. She was treated for alcohol addiction and her marriage to William Gorman later ended in divorce.[28]

During November 1962, Nogly organised a press conference for Bazna, in order to promote his book and his planned lawsuit. However, it was not a success and achieved little.

Bazna did try action against the German government, asking for a total of 1.7 million marks, but later reduced this by asking for a modest monthly pension, again with the same result. However, the story was covered by a TV documentary in Germany, the *Cicero Affair*, shown several times between 1963–64. Bazna stayed on in Germany, working as a night watchman in Munich.[29]

The great spy had rather missed the boat as far as publicity for Operation Cicero was concerned, with much interest attracted by the sensational film *Five Fingers* in 1952. By the time Bazna's story emerged, the new generation growing up in Germany wanted to forget the war. Even the various British security services treated him and his book with contempt, dismissing his effort as 'almost wholly imaginary'.[30]

# 22

# STELLAR SPY

Cicero was described by David Kahn as a 'Stellar Spy' amongst the ranks of German spies in the Second World War;[1] Fitzroy MacLean wrote that Cicero was a spy who 'really did deliver the goods'; and Richard Wires thought him the 'most successful spy of World War II'.[2] But does he deserve this praise?

Cicero's career, albeit short, did present the Germans with a unique opportunity to cause damage to the Allied cause, with MI6 later admitting 'the potential damage was enormous'.[3] Yet even with the impressive array of documents supplied to the Germans, the Allies suffered little damage as a result, as the Nazi leaders failed to use this windfall of secret information to affect the outcome of the war.

In many ways, Cicero was a spy from another era. He was an amateur with no intelligence training and, as such, his overriding motive was financial gain, so the Germans naturally mistrusted him. The British, for their part, never considered him, a lowly valet, as a possible threat because he was 'too stupid'.[4]

Bazna-Cicero remained in control of what he did throughout; as a 'walk-in' he merely made the offer, and if the Germans turned him down he would go elsewhere. Juan Pujol Garcia, codenamed Garbo, Britain's most famous and effective spy, was also a 'walk-in', but he was motivated by his hatred for the fascists developed during the Spanish Civil War. A double agent, he was controlled by the British and trained to some degree by both sides.

Bazna was an Albanian, although he often claimed to be Turkish, and lived most of his life in Turkey. He went by several first names – Elyesa, Diello and Ilya – and used Pierre as a cover name when contacting the Germans by telephone. Many, not only Moyzisch, thought him older than he was. His baldness and worldly experience contributed to this, coupled with his ability to blend into the background unnoticed.

Operation Cicero was simple in that it primarily involved only two men, after Bazna's initial approach to the Jenkes, who he had worked for briefly before. Von Papen, who never met Cicero, made the decision of handing the affair over to Moyzisch and the SD, rather than the *Abwehr*, which he favoured, merely because he thought it might cause trouble. By then the *Abwehr* was badly compromised through its leaks to the British, and Cicero would have soon been revealed to GCHQ, who had been reading its signals since the end of 1941. Dilly Knox from Bletchley Park, a brilliant classical scholar, papyrologist and cryptographer, who in 1917 succeeded in breaking much of the German naval code, had also cracked the *Abwehr* code.[5] The German military intelligence service used a subtly different Enigma machine, but Knox broke it working largely from home while ill. Sadly, he died of stomach cancer in 1943.[6]

Unlike most espionage stories, there was no violence involved. At times, according to Moyzisch, Cicero did carry a gun. As Cicero explains:'I don't intend to let them catch me alive.'[7] This may have been a device by Moyzisch to heighten excitement in his narrative. However, the risk of violence or even death must have been ever present during their clandestine meetings, and at the British Embassy should Bazna be discovered.

Moyzisch proved a capable handler, despite having little experience of field operations. He did fail to make arrangements to contact Cicero in an emergency, though neither Moyzisch nor his superiors in Berlin had any means to direct or control Cicero, and had he been pushed too hard then the cagey agent was likely to go elsewhere.

Schellenberg supported Moyzisch well, taking the Cicero documents seriously right from the start, and making sure all were thoroughly investigated by experts. While Kaltenbrunner and Ribbentrop were consumed by personal squabbles, Schellenberg remained largely frustrated as his detailed intelligence reports were wasted by the Nazi High Command.[8]

The end date of Cicero's espionage activities is not clear, though Moyzisch and Bazna tried to link the end to the defection of Cornelia Kapp in April 1944. It is likely Bazna had stopped before that, in March, and the Vermehrens' defection may have had more effect on his decision. Sir Hughe, the British ambassador, was away for a large part of March, thus removing the opportunity to spy. It is unlikely Bazna would have resumed when the ambassador returned, as the risk would have been too great. Bazna says he left on the last day of April 1944, which would have been a Sunday.[9] Some sources say he was sacked, although it is more likely that Bazna gave up spying in early March and left his employment at the British Embassy without trouble.

Just how many British top secret documents did end up in Berlin as a result of Cicero's activities? Moyzisch says he purchased forty to fifty rolls of film, amounting to some 400 photographs,[10] while Maria Molkenteller says she translated 120–150 Cicero documents.[11] More than one photograph would have been taken of single papers so the difference in the amount between Moyzisch and Molkenteller is not significant.

The range of topics covered by the documents was fairly wide. The most significant were about Allied plans for the future strategy of the war at a very high level. Sir Hughe was often involved in this, or kept well informed of developments by the Foreign Office. The documents revealed the tensions between the Allied powers, and the future of Turkey as an Allied partner was of particular interest. A number of military operations were also mentioned, such as: the air raid on Sofia; Operation Saturn, the movement of RAF squadrons to Turkish air bases, and the later 'Accolade' and 'Anvil' bombing operations; the use of submarines in the Black Sea;[12] and details of the Allied invasion of Europe, such as the codename Overlord and the likely embarkation date of spring 1944.

The fact the Nazi leadership failed to make use of the material, by first understandably doubting Cicero, and later not using the material to guide their own strategy, does not devalue the material supplied or the seriousness of the catastrophic breach of British security. The gods of war smiled kindly on the British and they suffered no real damage, other than to their prestige after the war.

The British were both lucky and unlucky in having Sir Hughe Knatchbull-Hugessen as their ambassador in Ankara during the war. He was a charming and gregarious ambassador, and carried out his duties with dedication and consummate skill, but his personal habits made him a security liability. He largely ignored advice from his security staff, often because of personal prejudices, and failed to follow basic procedure over document security.

Even when warned in January by the Dulles reports from Switzerland, British security failed to catch Cicero, or even worse to seal the leaks. Sir Hughe, to a degree, misled the investigation by laying the blame on the Turks.

Later the American OSS 'played a hidden strange role'.[13] The relatively new organisation in Turkey appeared more interested in exposing and embarrassing the SIS branch by withholding vital information from them, rather than working together against the Axis powers. However, the various British security services did not always operate in harmony. Ex-MI5 man, Peter Wright, wrote: 'The most serious lack of liaison was undoubtedly that between MI5 and GCHQ.'[14]

While in Turkey, and with some justification, MI6 found the Americans too eager to use locals with dubious loyalties. Thus the two services did not trust each other. The OSS branch in Turkey should have informed MI6 that a British Embassy servant was a spy, and the fact they did not was inexcusable. By the time Cornelia Kapp was in British hands and was being interrogated in Cairo, Cicero had long gone.

Kapp would have been difficult for the OSS to handle and evaluate when she first approached them in Ankara.[15] Her bad nerves, which were not an act and continued in later life, made her poorly suited for her role as a spy at the German Embassy. However, soon enough the Americans had a clear enough picture to have warned the British. The fact that they did not largely devalued the information she had obtained.

Cicero certainly had a fair degree of good luck in his four-month career: he never aroused suspicion, even when security was tightened; he continued to work, though the quality of the documents he supplied was not as good; and by March, with access to documents much restricted, and the heightened fear of being caught, he stopped spying and literally walked away.

The payment of £300,000 sterling that Bazna received for his spying activities raises two questions. How much was counterfeit? And why did Bazna not become suspicious that the payment he was receiving was too easy to obtain? Schellenberg thought that maybe only half the notes paid out were counterfeit, despite the fact that, when Kaltenbrunner took over the case, he sent £200,000 in forged notes to Ankara.[16] Including the first payment of £20,000, Moyzisch felt Cicero was paid about £40,000 in genuine money and goods: about £35,000 in good sterling notes, the $20,000 dollars and £2,000 in diamonds Moyzisch had obtained for him.[17] It was while changing some sterling into dollars for Cicero that Moyzisch first learnt that his agent was being paid largely in counterfeit money.

It was not until much later that Cicero realised anything was wrong. He was too clever for his own good, believing he controlled everything;

and he was slow in exchanging the money and simply stockpiled it in his room at the British Embassy. For a man possessed of a fair degree of basic cunning, he was all too easily duped in this respect, and he was even surprised by the amount the Germans were willing to part with. They later reduced the scale of payment so as to not arouse suspicion and to impress on Cicero that funds were limited, whereas they had plenty of counterfeit notes.

The Allies and the Axis used Turkey as an espionage battleground. Turkey was the goal; she supplied vital war materials to the Germans and controlled important shipping routes that lay across vital areas for the warring powers. Axis forces controlled Greece, the Aegean and much of the Balkans. To the north was the ever-present menace of the Soviet Union, always mistrusted by the Turkish, and the Western Allies controlled the Mediterranean to the south. The Cicero documents were instrumental in German attempts to keep Turkey neutral and frustrating British aims to use Turkish air and naval bases. It is apparent that the Cicero information in itself, or Von Papen's use of it in trying to bully the Turks, did not overly influence them, though the documents did keep the Germans informed of the lack of British progress.

Naturally, the Turkish leaders acted in the best interests of their country: they felt they had been duped by the Germans in the First World War and had no wish to be in the Second World War by either side. At the December meeting in Cairo they identified that the British 'Turkey' policy, after their defeat in the Aegean campaign, had been largely discounted by the Americans. This resulted in the Turkish policy of 'sitting on the fence', which in the end was perhaps too prolonged and did favour the Germans, and finally undermined Turkey's own ability to affect the Allied war plans.

What advantage did the Germans gain from the Cicero documents? Moyzisch felt that:

> In the long run all that the German leaders learned from these documents was simply that they were about to lose the war.[18]

However, Von Papen disagreed with this:

> ... the Cicero information was immensely valuable for two reasons.
> We obtained indisputable evidence of Turkey's attitude to increasing Allied pressure. We also learnt that the possibility of an Allied attack in

the Balkans through Salonica could be ruled out. This was of great importance, because it meant there was no need for the considerable dispersal of our defensive forces which the indifferent communications in this region would otherwise have made necessary. The Supreme Command now realized that the only real threat with which it had to contend was the invasion of France, although our knowledge of Operation Overlord was limited to the name. (I repeatedly suggested that in order to deceive the enemy into thinking that we knew its details, our propaganda should give the impression that we possessed considerable knowledge of Overlord. However, for some reason Hitler declined to allow this.)[19]

Ultimately, the Cicero documents did not give the Germans any clear information on Allied military thinking, but they did indicate that the next major Anglo-American move would come in the west and not in the Aegean or the Balkans. This was quickly overshadowed by the unrest in the Axis satellites in Eastern Europe and the unstable Eastern Front against the Russians.

The German High Command missed the opportunity to shift troops from this region largely because of Hitler's fears over these developments, but these divisions in the main were left to wither on the vine and many were cut off later in the war. The Germans were further hoodwinked by Operation Fortitude into considering Allied landings in Norway or the South of France, and, as a result, hundreds of thousands of German troops were left in these areas.

The German intelligence services during the war were, on the whole, pretty poor. The *Abwehr* had scored some early successes, but its signal traffic was quickly read when the people at Bletchley Park broke their codes. It also became an organisation filled with people in opposition to the Nazi regime. While the Nazi leadership schemed against each other, as Schellenberg did to have Ribbentrop removed from his post as Foreign Minister, much good information fell to petty squabbles. This is largely what happened to the Germans' greatest intelligence success, that stellar spy, Cicero.

# 23

# CICERO IN FICTION

'Really first-rate spies are, like really first-rate musicians, rare. No country has as many of either as it would like.' So wrote Eric Ambler in *The Mask of Dimitrios*.[1]

The CIA released 'Footnote to Cicero' in 1994 and called Operation Cicero 'a textbook exercise in tradecraft' and a 'nice, neat package to handle, uncomplicated by consequences and relatively free of loose ends'.[2]

It hardly seems that Bazna was a 'first-rate spy', as he was more the amateur opportunist, and the case was hardly 'free of loose ends' for those who took part, which may be part of the reason the story has not figured in fiction that prominently. Compared to 'Operation Kondor' and 'The Rebecca Code', which features in three novels, three feature films and numerous articles, Operation Cicero seems largely to have disappeared.[3]

The feature film *Five Fingers* is the most fictionalised treatment of the story, even if it claims to be true. The advertising trailer tells the audience that the exteriors were filmed in Turkey and the events depicted were 'True, Every Startling Moment'. Yet the credits say the film is 'Based on a novel by L.C. Moyzisch'.[4] Michael Wilson knew the film would be made in the semi-documentary style of the 1940s, and they were bringing a recently discovered espionage story to the screen. Nevertheless, above all, they needed to embrace a story that gripped the audience; the story needed more appeal, which was brought about by the introduction of new fictional characters and a good dose of fictional events. There is no real violence in the film, as Mankiewicz observed it only needed 'humour, sex and excitement', and the main themes centred on deception and betrayal.

The anti-hero, known as Diello, is frustrated by the sexual promise of Countess Anna, a French-born Polish aristocrat, played by the beautiful French actress Danielle Darrieux. She completely outwits Diello in stealing his money, obtained by spying on his employers, the British. Both fall victim to human folly; all is deception, double-dealing and treachery.[5]

The film distorts most of the principal characters. Diello, played by James Mason, is a wonderful depiction of a glamorised servant-spy; a cynical lecher-type and a distortion of P.G. Wodehouse's Jeeves. None of his highly polished performance could possibly derive from Bazna, whose base characteristic was low cunning and an ability to appear inconspicuous to those in authority around him.

Moyzisch, played by Oscar Karlweis, is a bumbling idiot who is easily manipulated by Diello. Michael Rennie, the English-born actor who sounds American, perhaps best known for playing the alien visitor Klaatu in the science fiction film *The Day the Earth Stood Still*, plays George Travis, another totally inept security man on the British side. He only realises what is going on too late to retrieve the situation. Sir Hughe becomes Sir Frederic and is played by Walter Hampden as some kindly uncle. The SD send in Colonel Von Richter, an ardent Nazi, to find out more about Cicero; he is played by Herbert Berghof in a suitably menacing style. Maybe only John Wengraf, playing Franz Von Papen, achieves something like the right depiction of the skilful diplomat. The inept supporting characters do enhance the roles of Cicero and Anna, the spy's unlikely confederate, but their deception of the Allies, and each other, finally receives ultimate justice in a memorable ending.

*Five Fingers* did promote the idea that Cicero had obtained details of the Allied invasion plans for Overlord. However, in the film, the Germans fail to realise what they have, believing it to be a plant, and destroy the documents. Thus the Allies escape disaster by luck, which heightened the appeal of the film in dramatic terms.

Why the film was called *Five Fingers* is unknown. Zanuck thought it suggested a hand perhaps clutching money, a symbol of greed, but it was not used in this way even in the trailers. Of course it might go back to fingers appearing on one of the photographs taken by Cicero. James Mason felt Zanuck would not use 'Cicero' in the title because the American audience might confuse it with a suburb of Chicago, well known as 'a hotbed of gangsters'.[6]

The film opens with questions being asked in the British Parliament. Then Cicero's working period is confined to a short period in the spring of 1944.

The opening scenes proper show Von Papen at a diplomatic reception in Ankara, where he meets the beauty Countess Anna Straviska, who has suffered great property and financial losses, which she attributes to the

Germans, making her a refugee in a foreign land. However, she offers to spy for Germany as she is accepted by all sides. Von Papen turns down her offer. Moyzisch is introduced to her and is clearly attracted to Anna, but is told by her he cannot afford her.

Returning to the embassy, Moyzisch is approached by a stranger offering to sell him photographs of secret documents. He sets his terms saying he will telephone Moyzisch in three days to see if he is interested and he will use the code-name 'Pierre'.

The stranger returns to the British Embassy where it is revealed he is Diello, the British Ambassador's valet; it is also revealed he once worked for Countess Straviska's late husband.

Back at the German Embassy, the signal comes from Berlin agreeing to use the man, and that Ribbentrop codenamed him Cicero. Von Papen treats this with scorn, surprised that Ribbentrop had ever heard of Cicero.

At their second meeting, Cicero delivers two film rolls. Moyzisch takes them to the dark room; on his return he finds Cicero has opened the safe and is counting his money. He has done this, he says, by guessing the safe combination has something to do with Hitler (there is a bust of the Führer in the room); in this case the combination is the date he came to power, which Cicero says was rather obvious.

In a dingy part of town Cicero visits Anna, who is living in poor circumstances; he offers to fund a new wealthy style of life for her and in return she will rent a large villa where behind closed doors he can conduct his business. She will also hold the funds there in a safe, as he cannot keep it or bank the money. A sexual attraction fuelled by greed begins between the two.

While in Berlin Moyzisch is interviewed by Kaltenbrunner and Colonel Von Richter. Both suspect the documents are a trap, but wait for the Allied bombing of Romanian oil fields mentioned in them. Von Papen is furious when he learns of this and that the Romanians had not been warned, calling the Nazi leaders a 'Government of juvenile delinquents'.

Von Richter is sent to Ankara to take over dealing with Cicero. A security agent George Travers arrives at the same time to investigate the leak at the British Embassy. Having been alerted by decoding German signals. Travers soon believes the leaks are the result of gossip.

At Countess Straviska's villa Von Richter meets Cicero, who tells him it is a good idea for him to take over as Moyzisch is 'not very bright'. The colonel tries to find out Cicero's motive, but all he will say is that his aim is purely to be wealthy. Indeed, he does not even expect Germany to win the war. Richter tells him previous documents have mentioned Overlord; he offers him £40,000 if he can obtain details of these, where and when the Allies will land.

However, with new electronic safe alarms installed at the British Embassy, Cicero feels it is best to bow out with the £130,000 he already has, although he has agreed to meet Richter again, but this time at the Haci Bayram Mosque. Moyzisch and Richter go there and wait but Cicero does not turn up.

Cicero tells Anna they will retire to Brazil – his money is his own but he will look after her. She is not impressed with this but hides her feelings. Meanwhile, she has obtained passports and documents for them as man and wife.

The next day, back at the British Embassy, Travis mentions that Countess Straviska has left Ankara with £130,000 and gone to Switzerland; Cicero hears this and is shocked. He also notices a letter to the ambassador in Anna's handwriting. Sir Frederic is away at a meeting in Cairo, but he cannot open it or hide it before it is locked away in the safe. Travis has begun to suspect Cicero and has him followed. Diello tries to trace Anna and realises he is being watched.

By telephone, Cicero contacts Moyzisch saying he will get the invasion plans, but will deliver them in Istanbul and the price has gone up to £100,000.

By removing a fuse from the main fuse box, Cicero learns how to deactivate the alarm and open the safe, which he does, removing Anna's letter still unread, and he photographs some of the documents.

However, on the same floor of the building a maid going about her cleaning duties finds her vacuum cleaner will not work; she finds a fuse missing in the fuse box and replaces it. Placing the papers back in the safe and closing the door, Cicero activates the alarm. In the resulting confusion he is able to leave the building saying he is chasing someone.

Travers orders his colleagues to kill Diello if possible. Both sides wait for him at the main station. However, Cicero evades them and boards the train as they do. Alone in his compartment, he reads Anna's letter to Sir Frederic in which she denounces him as a German spy. He destroys the letter, throwing it out of the window.

Money and rolls of film are exchanged in an Istanbul restaurant. Both sides have agents there watching each other. Roles are now reversed: the Germans want to kill him, while the British need to interrogate him. He accepts British protection, but outside in the street he loses them and the following Germans in a passing funeral procession. With his knowledge of the city neither side can find him.

In the German consulate in Istanbul Moyzisch develops the film. Meanwhile, Richter receives a message from Von Papen: the ambassador has a letter from Anna stating Cicero is a British plant, and he believes her. Moyzisch still thinks the documents are genuine. However, Richter tears up the developed prints, throwing the pieces out of the window. The window faces the harbour where Cicero joins a ship bound for South America.

The last scene shows Diello dressed in a white dinner jacket at his villa overlooking Rio de Janeiro. There two officials visit saying the pounds he had been using in Brazil are counterfeit and they were made in Germany during the war. Similar notes had turned up in Turkey and Switzerland; there they had been traced to a Polish lady.

The irony strikes Diello, who bursts out laughing much to the horror of the two officials who point out this is a serious matter. But he is consumed with laughter while tossing pound notes into the air, where they are whisked away by the wind, while he shouts out Anna's name several times.[7]

*Five Fingers* received good reviews on its release in February 1952: *The Times* called it 'unfailingly entertaining' and The *Time Out Film Guide*, 'An elegantly witty espionage movie'.[8] The film was profitable at the box office.

To obtain the much-coveted part of Erwin Rommel in Twentieth Century Fox's *The Desert Fox*, James Mason had to sign on with that studio for two years. It was something he was not keen on, but the lure of playing Rommel was too strong, so he duly signed with the caveat that he had some say on the other parts he might be called upon to play. However, he did not suffer 'a moment's indecision about the first offer', which was to play Cicero in *Five Fingers*.

Mason found Michael Wilson's screenplay 'excellent' and he felt the most 'original performance came from Oscar Karlweis who took the role of Moyzisch, the author of the book, who ironically became the butt of the Wilson/Mankiewicz humour'. Even years after its release, Mason found he still admired it and could watch it as 'one of the few films in which I appear which can be relied on to hold my attention throughout'.[9]

In the account by Moyzisch, and particularly Bazna, there are elements of fiction. For instance, in his handling of Cornelia Kapp, Moyzisch is anything but frank, claiming he never really understood her, although he did admit she 'tricked me, and did it most cleverly'.[10] He tried to mini-mise her overall effect, only conceding she might have copied a few pages of secret documents. He felt her turning was down to the British, maybe through the two German deserters who he said later tried to get him to defect to the British. Von Papen also saw some development like this as inevitable, and it was 'interesting that Moyzisch's own secretary' was the one who 'deserted to the British'.[11] There is no doubt that Moyzisch tried to enhance his role, too, often referring to himself as a diplomat, which he was not, and hiding Kapp's real identity, not so much to protect her or her father, but to protect his own reputation. Kapp also exaggerated her own importance, indicating frequent meetings with OSS agents, and the amount of secret material she saw and supplied them with.[12]

Bazna also felt, after receiving Seiler's tapes, that Kapp had defected to the British,[13] although he is prone to more clear flights of fantasy. Also we must question his ability to recognise the face of the driver who had tailed Moyzisch's car through Ankara as being the man he saw weeks later with Kapp in the Ankara Palace Hotel.[14]

His story about buying a car from Busk, First Secretary at the British Embassy, is also dubious. By then the war was over and Busk would have been well aware of Bazna's identity. Busk supposedly advertised the car for sale in a local newspaper and Bazna recognised the telephone number. They met and Busk invited him in, making 'polite inquiries after my health'. Bazna told him he was well. While examining the car he says he asked after Mara, who had been the Busks' nanny.

'Is she married?' he asked, closing the bonnet of the car.

Married to an American with a child of her own, replied Busk, and living in the United States.

He says he bought the car for £300 with the forged German £5 notes, although he had no idea about this at the time. This is all clearly fiction and yet another ruse to enhance his own reputation.[15]

***

159

The Cicero spy case has not been used directly in other fiction, although elements appear in some stories, such as Ian Fleming's 1957 book *From Russia with Love*. It has a defection from the Russians to the British with a love story at its heart, and much of the action takes place in Turkey and on trains.

It is doubtful whether Fleming would have come across Cicero during his time working at Naval Intelligence during the Second World War. However, it is more than likely he would have read Moyzisch's book and seen the film *Five Fingers*. He went to Istanbul in 1956 to cover the Interpol conference. Darko Kenim, the extrovert Turkish Secret Service agent in *From Russia with Love*, was based on Nazum Kalkavan, Fleming's guide to the city.[16]

*From Russia with Love* would become Fleming's most successful book. The novel tells the story of Smersh (Death to Spies), the Soviet counter-intelligence department, and the attempt to take revenge on the British Secret Service by luring James Bond to Istanbul to meet the beautiful Tatiana Romanova, who apparently wants to defect. She would bring with her a 'Specktor' machine that could decipher Russian top secret radio traffic; this would be 'a priceless victory' and its loss to the Russians 'a major disaster'.[17]

Tatiana Romanova defects by leaving Turkey with Bond on board the Orient Express, just as Kapp was met by an American agent on board the express to Istanbul. Clearly Fleming based the 'Specktor' on the German Enigma machine, which he would have come across on his visits to Bletchley Park.[18] He had also been involved in various schemes, one of which was Operation Ruthless to capture an Enigma machine German naval codebook. There any similarities disappear and Fleming would have known nothing about Cornelia Kapp's flight when writing *From Russia with Love* in 1956, yet he would have been aware of the defection of Erich Vermehren and others in Turkey.

Fleming's *From Russia with Love* is arguably the best of the Bond books. It was one of President John F. Kennedy's favourite books – a fact that was outlined in a *Life* magazine article on the newly elected president, coming in at number nine of ten favourites stated. This did much for the books sales by Viking in the United States.[19]

★★★

Alistair MacLean's 1957 book, *The Guns of Navarone*, would seem to have little link with the Cicero case. However, the opening narration to the 1961 film by James Robertson Justice, who plays Captain James Jenson RN, an intelligence officer, tells us that:

> In 1943 the Axis powers decide that a show of strength might bully neutral Turkey into joining them. Their target is a command of 2,000 British soldiers marooned on the island of Keros in the Aegean Sea. Rescue by the Royal Navy is impossible because of large radar-directed guns on the nearby island of Navarone.

The Germans are soon expected to launch their assault, so a small, oddly assorted Commando team is sent in to destroy the guns that covered the narrow Maidos Straits: the story is well-known book and, later, film.[20]

More of the 'bullying' of Turkey could be said to have come from the Allied side in 1943, following the change of sides by Italy, and this is something the Western Allies might not have liked to admit to, even in 1961.

Leading Torpedo Operator Alistair MacLean, in his early twenties, visited the area in September 1944 aboard the *Dido* class cruiser HMS *Royalist*. The ship sank two blockade runners to the north of Suda Bay, Crete, and bombarded shore targets on other Greek islands; all good material for *The Guns of Navarone*.[21]

In 1958, MacLean wrote his thoughts on how the novel developed for the broadsheet of the Companion Book Club:

> I wanted to write a war story – with the accent on the story. Only a fool would pretend that there is anything noble or splendid about modern warfare but there is no denying that it provides a great abundance of material for a writer, provided no attempt is made either to glorify it or exploit its worst aspects. I think it was a perfectly legitimate territory for a story-teller. Personal experience, I suppose, helped to play some part in the location of this story. I spent some wartime months in and around Greece and the Aegean islands, although at no time, I must add, did I run the risk of anything worse than a severe case of sunburn, far less find myself exposed to circumstances such as those in which the book's characters find themselves.
>
> But I did come across and hear about, both in the Aegean and in Egypt, men to whom danger and the ever-present possibility of capture and death

were the very stuff of existence; these were the highly trained specialists of Earl Jellicoe's Special Boat Service and the men of the Long Range Desert Group, who had turned their attention to the Aegean islands after the fall of North Africa. Regularly these men were parachuted into enemy-held islands or came there by sea in the stormy darkness of a wind-and rain-filled night and operated, sometimes for months on end, as spies, saboteurs and liaison officers with resistance groups.

Some even had their own boats, based on German islands, and operated throughout the Aegean with conspicuous success and an almost miraculous immunity to capture and sinking.

It was against this background that Cicero started his work. In many ways, the failure of Churchill's ill-fated Aegean campaign made his work more important for the Germans as a window into Allied thinking about the Balkans and the Aegean. Of course, Alistair MacLean invented some of the locations in *The Guns of Navarone*:

Here obviously was excellent material for a story and it had the added advantage for the writer that it was set in an archipelago: I had the best of both worlds, the land and the sea, always ready to hand. But the determining factor in the choice of location and plot was neither material nor the islands themselves: that lay in the highly complicated political situation that existed in the islands at the time, and in the nature of Navarone itself. [A factor Winston Churchill tried to take advantage of in his ill-fated Aegean campaign.]

There is no such island as Navarone, but there were one or two islands remarkably like it, inasmuch as they were (a) German-held, (b) had large guns that dominated important channels and (c) had these guns so located as to be almost immune to destruction by the enemy. Again the situation in the Dodecanese islands was dangerous and perplexing in the extreme, as it was difficult to know from one month to another whether Germans, Greeks, British or Italians were in power there – an excellent setting for a story. So I moved a Navarone-type island from the middle of the Aegean to the Dodecanese, close to the coast of Turkey, placed another island, filled with trapped and apparently doomed British soldiers, just to the north of it, and took as much advantage as I could of what I had seen, what I heard, the fictitious geographical situation I had arranged for my own benefit, and the very real political and military state of affairs that existed in the Dodecanese at that time.[22]

In a number of ways, the exploits of Cicero and the people involved with him are as entertaining as those of the characters in Fleming's and MacLean's books. James Mason thought so, as he considered *Five Fingers* 'such a good film' and one of the most 'sensible' treatments of a spy story up to that time.[23]

# DRAMATIS PERSONAE

## Elyesa Bazna (Agent Cicero) (1904–70)

An Albanian/Turkish chauffeur, petty criminal, locksmith, taxi driver, valet, singer, who spied for the Germans. His book, *I was Cicero*, was published in 1962.

Born in Pristina, Kosovo, at that time part of the Turkish/Ottoman Empire, to Albanian parents, he moved with his family at a young age to Salonica, where he attended school. As a young man he moved to Istanbul. Arrested there as a petty criminal, when the city was occupied after the First World War by the Allies, he was taken to France and imprisoned in a labour camp near Marseilles. On his release he stayed in France and worked at the Berliet Motor Company, where he became a locksmith.

Returning to Istanbul, he became a taxi driver. Later he found a post as driver-servant for the Yugoslavian ambassador, moving on to become valet to a colonel at the US Embassy. In a similar post, in Ankara, he was employed by Herr Jenke at the German Embassy, but was dismissed for snooping and reading confidential embassy mail. He went on to become valet to Mr Busk, First Secretary at the British Embassy, before finally becoming valet to the British ambassador, Sir Hughe Knatchbull-Hugessen.

In October 1942 he started photographing secret documents in the British Embassy, which he decided to sell to the Germans. He approached Herr Jenke, who referred him to the SD man at the German Embassy, Ludwig Moyzisch. Bazna offered to supply secret British documents for cash, working initially for £20,000 for fifty-six documents photographed. The Germans gave him the codename 'Cicero'.

His motive was financial gain, although he enjoyed the feelings of power and danger. He confided to the Germans that he hated the British because a Briton had killed his father, but this was a lie.

Bazna relied on low cunning, intelligence and courage, combined with certain skills from his past, to obtain his ends. He spoke French and English, and probably German too, but he did not use this while working with the Germans, relying on French instead. He was happy to give up spying when things clearly became too dangerous, by which time he had accumulated £300,000 sterling. However, he was cheated by the Nazi's who paid him with counterfeit money.

British intelligence were warned by the Americans that there was a leak at their embassy in Ankara, but failed to discover Bazna was the spy. A new alarm system was installed at the embassy, and the defection of several Germans to the Allies led to Bazna giving up his brief spying career.

When Bazna began to use his counterfeit money in large amounts on business building projects, it was found to be forged and came to the attention of the Turkish authorities. He avoided imprisonment by the Turkish courts, who in the end believed his improbable story that in some way he had been duped by the Germans. Later, he tried to sue the West German government to recover the money, but was unsuccessful.

Bazna spent most of his later life in Istanbul running various small businesses; however, any profit went to pay his creditors. Later, with the aid of a German journalist, Hans Nogly, he published his memoirs of Operation Cicero.

Bazna lived in Munich for the last years of his life, working as a night watchman. He died aged 66 in December 1970.

# Adolf Burger (b. 1917)

A Slovak now living in Prague. Printer, typesetter and factory manager. His book, *The Devil's Workshop: A Memoir of the Nazi Counterfeiting Operation*, was published in 1983, and later filmed in 2008.

He was born into a Jewish family in Velka Lomnica, an ethnic German village, in what is now Slovakia. His father died when he was 4, but his mother later remarried a Christian, giving Adolf the status of a non-Jew. His siblings over the years managed to emigrate to the British mandate of Palestine. He did not join them and, in 1938, moved to work in Bratislava. His job as a printer, a valued occupation, kept him free of deportation to German concentration camps. However, at the request of the resistance he began to print fake baptismal certificates for Jews to avoid deportation. The certificates stated the holder had been Roman Catholic since birth. Burger's work was discovered and he was deported to Auschwitz with his wife in 1942.

His wife Gizela was killed later in 1942. After eighteen months at Auschwitz, his profession probably saved his life as he was selected for Operation Bernhard and transferred to Sachsenhausen concentration camp in April 1944, where he worked in the counterfeit workshop. Over a period of months the operation was transferred to several camps. Burger was finally liberated at Ebensee camp in May 1945.

Adolf Burger now lives in Prague. His book, *The Devils Workshop* was published in English in 2009. While in London for the book's launch he visited the Bank of England, where he was presented with one of the notes forged in Operation Bernhard sixty years before. His book was dramatised as *The Counterfeiters* in 2008 and received a foreign language Academy Award.

## Marcus Tullius Cicero (106 BC–43 BC)

Roman philosopher, politician, lawyer and orator.

Cicero was born in Arpinum, a hill town 60 miles south-east of Rome. He came from a wealthy municipal family of the Roman equestrian order.

He introduced the Roman's to the Greek schools of philosophy, and was an accomplished orator and lawyer, but he believed his political career to be his most important achievement. During his consulship, a Catilinarian conspiracy attempted to overthrow the government; Cicero suppressed the revolt and had its leaders executed without trial.

His most famous work, *De Republica* (*On the Commonwealth*), a dialogue on Roman politics, was written in six books between 54 and 51 BC.

During the first century BC, civil war plagued the country, resulting in the dictatorship of Gaius Julius Caesar. Cicero championed a return to republican government. Following the death of Julius Caesar, Cicero became the enemy of Mark Antony during the internecine power struggle, attacking him directly in a series of speeches. He was proscribed as an enemy of the state and murdered in 43 BC. To his murderers his last words were: 'There is nothing proper about what you are doing, soldier, but do try and kill me properly.'

## Allen Welsh Dulles (1893–1969)

United States lawyer, diplomat, intelligence officer, OSS Swiss office director, and director of the CIA 1953–61.

Dulles was born in Watertown, New York, in April 1893. He graduated from Princeton University and entered the diplomatic service in 1916. While working as a legal adviser to the US delegation to the League of Nations in the 1930s, he met Adolf Hitler and Benito Mussolini.

In 1935 he visited Germany on a business trip and was outraged by Nazi treatment of the Jews and dissidents. He moved to get the law firm he worked for, Sullivan and Cromwell, to close their Berlin office.

In Bern, Switzerland, during the Second World War, he was director of the OSS office. It was he who discovered, from information provided by Fritz Kolbe, a German diplomat and anti-Nazi who supplied vital secret German documents, the existence of Agent Cicero, which Dulles passed onto the British. Kolbe also supplied him with details regarding the Messerschmitt Me 262, the first operational jet fighter aircraft. He also received warnings from Kolbe about the V1 and V2 missile programmes.

The OSS was dissolved in 1945 and the CIA was brought into being by an act of the US Congress in 1947.

After a brief period in politics, Dulles became the director of the CIA in 1953 and helped modernise the US intelligence service. However, with the controversy surrounding the Bay of Pigs Affair he was dismissed by President John. F. Kennedy, but, ironically, was later reinstated by President Lyndon Johnson to investigate President Kennedy's murder

Dulles published his book, *The Craft of Intelligence*, in 1963. He died in 1969 of pneumonia.

## Ernst Kaltenbrunner (1903–46)

German lawyer; he joined the Nazi party in 1932 and the SS in 1935. Member of the Reichstag from 1938. In 1943 he was appointed chief of the RSHA.

Kaltenbrunner was born in Austria and attended Graz University, obtaining a law degree in 1926. Briefly he worked for law firms in Linz and Salzburg.

He was 6ft 7in tall and had a scarred face from duelling during his student days, although it is also suggested this might have been the result of a car accident.

He joined the Austrian Nazis in 1932. Imprisoned after the unsuccessful Nazi putsch in Vienna in 1934, he played a prominent role in the *Anschluss* (absorption of Austria into the German Reich) of 1938 and was promoted by Hitler to *SS-Gruppenführer*, equivalent to a lieutenant general in the army. In April 1941 he took over running the police. He succeeded Reinhard Heydrich after his assassination in May 1942 as head of the SD. Kaltenbrunner was in overall charge of the investigation into the aftermath of the July 1944 plot to kill Hitler, and the resulting mass executions of so-called traitors.

From the start, Kaltenbrunner had doubts about the 'Cicero documents', but he was more than willing to support Schellenberg's enthusiasm for them once he found out Ribbentrop, who he hated, mistrusted the agent.

Kaltenbrunner was arrested by US Troops in May 1945. He was the highest-ranking member of the SS to face trial at Nuremberg as, by that time, he was *SS-Obergruppenführer* (general) of the police and Waffen-SS. He tried to diminish his involvement in Nazi crimes, including the Holocaust, but he was condemned to death and hanged at Nuremberg in October 1946.

## Cornelia Kapp (Nele, Elisabet) (1919–?)

German nurse, German Embassy secretary, translator, OSS spy, and restaurant hostess.

Cornelia Kapp was brought up in Germany, India and the United States, as her father, Karl Kapp, was a German diplomat. He was consul general in Cleveland from 1936–41.

Cornelia went to school and university in Cleveland. She fell in love with a young American at university which changed her outlook on life.

In July 1941 the US government closed all German consulates, and the Kapps returned home to Germany which was a culture shock for Cornelia. Karl Kapp was posted to Italy while his daughter studied nursing in Germany. When her father was posted to Bulgaria in 1943, she went with him and became an embassy secretary in Sofia. She moved to a post in the German Embassy at Ankara to escape the bombing of Bulgaria; there she worked for L.C. Moyzisch of the SD.

According to the CIA while in Ankara she approached the OSS with an offer to spy for them, her sole motive was to return to the USA. Although it is possible she may have first been approached in Sofia by the OSS; however at that time the Americans had only recently opened their intelligence headquarters in Cairo and their Istanbul office was not running until April 1943.

Shortly after the defection of Erich Vermehren to the British, she defected to the Americans who handed her over to the British in Cairo. By 1944 Cornelia Kapp was in the USA. After the war she was in Chicago boarding with a family of German origin. She was visited there regularly by the FBI. Later she married an FBI man and moved to California.


## Sir Hughe Knatchbull-Hugessen KCMG (1886–1971)

British diplomat, civil servant and author.

He attended Eton and Oxford University, where he began a life-long friendship with Anthony Eden, Foreign Secretary during the Second World War and, later, prime minister. He graduated as a Bachelor of Arts in 1907, then he joined the Foreign Office in 1909. He married Mary Gilmour in 1912 and they had three children.

He served in the contraband service during the First World War, helping to enforce the blockade against Germany. In 1919 he was attached to the British delegation at the Versailles Conference.

He was a counsellor at the embassy in Brussels 1926–30, and envoy to Estonia, Lithuania and Latvia 1931–34. In 1936 he was sent to China as ambassador. In 1937 his car was strafed by a Japanese fighter aircraft; he was badly wounded and invalided home to Britain. It took him over a year to recover from his injuries.

In 1939 he was appointed ambassador to Turkey at Ankara. He had visited the country many times before and had been minister to Persia 1934–36. In Ankara he employed Elyesa Bazna as his valet, who opened his mail and safe, photographed the documents and sold them to the Germans as Agent Cicero.

In 1944 Sir Hughe was appointed ambassador to Belgium and Luxemburg, retiring from his post and the Foreign Office in 1947.

He was humiliated by the scandal of the Cicero Affair, which broke in 1950, and he was publicly rebuked in Parliament by the Foreign Secretary, Ernest Bevin. His poor attitude to security led directly to tempting Bazna into spying for the Germans. Through the rest of his life he made little comment on the 'Cicero Case' and chose to maintain a dignified silence.

# James Mason (1909–84)

British stage and screen actor.

James Mason was born in the West Riding of Yorkshire, and his father was a wealthy merchant. He was educated at Marlborough College and studied architecture at Cambridge. He joined the Old Vic Theatre in London, but had no formal training as an actor.

In 1933 Alexander Korda gave him a small role in *The Private Life of Don Juan*, but sacked him a few days later.

During the Second World War he registered as a conscientious objector, and this action estranged him from his family for many years. It is ironic, therefore, that his most famous role should be that of Erwin Rommel in *The Desert Fox*.

In the 1940s he starred in a series of Gainsborough melodramas, including *The Man in Grey* (1943) and *The Wicked Lady* (1945). These roles brought him to the attention of Hollywood producers. There his roles included Brutus in *Julius Caesar* (1953), and Erwin Rommel in *The Desert Fox* (1951). In 1952 he starred as 'Cicero' in *Five Fingers*. He went on to star in *20,000 Leagues under the Sea* (1954), *North by Northwest* (1959) and *Journey to the Centre of the Earth* (1959).

In 1952 he purchased a house which had once belonged to Buster Keaton, and there he found some old films which were decomposing;

he had them transferred to safety stock, including the great comedian in
*The Boat* (1921).

He was married to the British actress Pamela Ostrer from 1941–64,
and then to Australian actress Clarissa Kaye from 1971 until his death.
He died of a heart attack in 1984 aged 75. His ashes were buried in Vaud,
Switzerland, near the remains of his old friend, Charlie Chaplin.

The part of 'Cicero' in *Five Fingers* was one of his favourite roles. He
was nominated for three Academy Awards and three Golden Globes
(winning once).

## Sir Stewart Graham Menzies KCB, KCMG, DSO, MC (1890–1968)

British soldier, MI6 officer, assistant director, head of MI6 (1939–52).

Born in London into a wealthy family, his father John Graham Menzies
squandered much of the family fortune.

Stewart went to Eton College and then joined the Grenadier Guards.
During the First World War he was wounded at Zandvoorde in 1914,
and also fought at the First Battle of Ypres. In December 1914 he was
awarded the DSO. At the Second Battle of Ypres he was seriously injured
in a gas attack, and was discharged from active service due to his wounds.
He then joined the intelligence service, SIS. He was a member of the
British delegation to the 1919 Versailles Conference.

In 1924 he was implicated in the forgery of the Zinoviev letter, in
an attempt to ensure a Conservative victory in the general election and
ending the first Labour government. He allowed much of the blame to
fall on Sidney Reilly; however Menzies later admitted sending the letter
to the *Daily Mail*.

In 1939, after the death of Admiral Hugh Sinclair, Menzies was
appointed chief of the SIS. The intelligence service and counter-intelligence was vastly extended under him, and the GC & CS at Bletchley
Park also came under his remit. He considered SOE to be amateurs. He
supported attempts to aid and control anti-Nazi groups in Germany,
including Admiral Wilhelm Canaris, head of the *Abwehr*.

Menzies was promoted to major general in 1944. After the war, SIS
was reorganised for the Cold War. He retired from the service in 1952,

after which the scandal broke that Kim Philby was a Soviet spy, which tarnished Menzies' reputation.

His efforts in the Second World War were a major factor in Allied victory. According to the writer Anthony Cave Brown, who knew Menzies well, he indicated that 'Cicero' had been a British double agent. This clearly was untrue, as Menzie's was never directly involved with the Cicero case.

Menzies was married three times and had one daughter by his second wife.


# Ludwig Carl Moyzisch (1902–?)

German/Austrian civil servant, SD officer, commercial attaché at German Embassy in Ankara, businessman and author.

Moyzisch was born in Vienna in 1902 and attended a technical school. He first worked as a contract writer for the Austrian government. In 1932 he joined the Austrian Nazi party, and later claimed he was sacked from his government post for his fascist activities.

In 1942, while in Ankara, Moyzisch applied to become a full member of the SS, but was turned down as he was unable to prove the identity of his mother's father and that he was 100 per cent Aryan.

Throughout the Cicero affair he was the main link to Bazna, conducting all the transactions and developing the films.

At the end of the Second World War he was extensively questioned by the British, during which he claimed to be Jewish. He was also called upon to give evidence at the Nuremberg Trials, but no charge was ever brought against him.

After the war he returned home to Austria with his family, settling in the Tyrol, near Innsbruck, where he became the export manager of a textile firm.

In 1950 his book, *Operation Cicero*, was published, revealing the story to the world. Sixteen years after the war's end, he met Bazna again, who he thought had been killed by the British. Hans Nogly, who helped Bazna write his book, arranged the meeting in order to corroborate the story he had been told. Moyzisch confirmed that Bazna had, indeed, been Cicero.

# Franz Joseph Von Papen (1879—1969)

German nobleman, soldier, intelligence agent, politician, chancellor of Germany, vice chancellor of Germany and diplomat.

Born into a noble Catholic family in Westphalia, he was educated as an army officer before joining the German General Staff in 1913. Shortly afterwards he moved to the diplomatic service, becoming military atta-ché to the German ambassador in the USA. In 1915 he was expelled from the United States for espionage activities and sabotage. Later, in the First World War, he served on the Western Front. In 1917 he joined the General Staff in the Middle East and served as a major in the Ottoman Army.

After the war he entered politics, becoming an MP for Prussia from 1921—32. In 1932 President Paul Von Hindenburg appointed him chan-cellor. Many observers at the time felt his appointment was a mistake, as he was too fond of intrigue. The French ambassador commented: 'Papen enjoyed the peculiarity of being taken seriously by neither his friends nor his enemies'. Another contemporary politician described him as 'a character from Alice in Wonderland'. However, at the International Conference on Reparations at Lausanne, he got the German debts reduced to a final payment of 3 billion marks, although the payment was never made. As chancellor he was compromised and had little sup-port in the Reichstag. He called an election in 1932 in the hope of gaining support; instead, the Nazi's became the largest party. Another election followed months later. Von Papen tried to negotiate with Hitler to stay in power, but found it impossible and resigned. In 1933 Hitler was appointed chancellor and Von Papen as vice chancellor.

Von Papen had hoped to control Hitler, but he was soon marginalised. In a speech at the University of Marburg, Von Papen called for an end to the SA terror in the streets. This infuriated Hitler, but he knew Von Papen had the support of Hindenburg, who could still call on the army to remove him from power. Thus came about 'The Night of the Long Knives', when Hitler purged the SA leadership and eliminated many political opponents, though Von Papen survived.

Shortly afterwards Hitler appointed Von Papen as German ambas-sador in Vienna. He helped bring about the *Anschluss* (annexation by Germany of Austria), which came about in March 1938.

In 1939 Von Papen was appointed as ambassador to Turkey. There he survived an assassination attempt in February 1942 by Soviet NKVD agents. He was highly involved in the Cicero affair, although never met the agent. He used the British top secret documents to keep Turkey out of the war and maintain vital chrome supplies to Germany until 1945.

In August 1944 he returned to Germany and had his last meeting with Hitler. He was captured by the US Army in April 1945. He was a defendant at the Nuremberg Trials, where he was later acquitted of all charges. He was sentenced to eight years' hard labour by the West German denazification court, but was released in 1949.

With the release of Moyzisch's book, *Operation Cicero*, Von Papen wrote a postscript to the English edition in support of the account. He also published a number of books and memoirs defending his actions during the critical period in German history from 1930–33, and outlining his part in the Cicero case.

He died in Obersasbach, West Germany, in 1969 aged 89.

## Joachim Von Ribbentrop (1893–1946)

German businessman, soldier, wine salesman, diplomat, and Foreign Minister of Nazi Germany.

Ribbentrop was born in Wesel, Prussia, and later attended French courses at a school in Metz. He became fluent in French and English, and lived at various times in France and England, before going to Canada in 1910. There he worked in banks and for various railway companies. With the outbreak of the First World War he returned to Germany via the USA.

Once back in Germany he enlisted in the German Army. He served on both the Eastern and Western fronts, and in Turkey, where he met Franz Von Papen. In 1919 he married into a wealthy Wiesbaden wine-producing family, and travelled extensively in Europe as their main salesman. In 1925 his aunt, Gertrude Von Ribbentrop, adopted him, which allowed him to add the aristocratic 'Von' to his name.

In 1928 he met Adolf Hitler and became his foreign policy adviser, later helping Hitler to be appointed chancellor. Ribbentrop was appointed ambassador to Britain in 1936, and became Reich Foreign Minister in 1938.

Ribbentrop played a key role in cementing the Pact of Steel with Italy, and the Soviet-German non-aggression pact, which sealed the fate of Poland. However, after 1941, his influence declined and his diplomatic record was one of failure.

He never trusted the Cicero documents, mainly because of his hatred of Kaltenbrunner and mistrust of Von Papen, who both supported them.

He was arrested in June 1945 and convicted of war crimes at the Nuremberg Trials. He was hanged in October 1946.

## Walther Friedrich Schellenberg (1910–52)

German intelligence officer, *SS-Brigadeführer*, head of the SD and author.

Schellenberg was born in Saarbucken, Germany, in 1910, the seventh child of a piano manufacturer; he was one of the youngest members of that generation of middle-class German men who were too young to have fought in the First World War. He attended university at Marburg and Bonn, studying medicine, but later switched to law. After graduating he joined the SS in May 1933.

The SD was founded in 1931 and led by the former naval officer Reinhard Heydrich, who built it up into a powerful surveillance and information-gathering agency. Schellenberg proved to be one of his most effective agents. He was used on foreign assignments, most spectacularly in the abduction of two British secret service agents from the Dutch border town of Venlo in November 1939, and in the arrest and interrogation of the Yugoslavian military attaché in Berlin in April 1941. In this way he came to the attention of Hitler, who often took a keen interest in such escapades.

From 1939–42 he was Heinrich Himmler's personal aide and deputy chief of the RSHA. In 1940 he compiled a blueprint for the occupation of Britain, published as *The Gestapo handbook for the Invasion of Britain*.

In 1942 he took over running Amt VI, the Foreign Intelligence Department of the SD. From the start he supported the Cicero documents as authentic. With the fall of his friend Admiral Wilhelm Canaris, who had been head of the *Abwehr*, he took over that organisation and incorporated it into the SD.

In 1945 he encouraged Himmler to overthrow Hitler and seek a separate peace with the Western Allies. He surrendered to the British in June and was subjected to a lengthy interrogation by MI5/MI6.

Schellenberg testified at the Nuremberg Trials, but did not face charges himself. He was convicted by the West Germany denazification court and sentenced to six years' imprisonment. During this time he wrote his memoirs, which were published in 1956.

He was released in 1951 due to ill health and moved to Switzerland, then to Lake Garda in Italy. He died of liver cancer in 1952 aged 42.

# FILMOGRAPHY

*Five Fingers*

Distributed by Twentieth Century Fox, 1952
Running time 103 minutes in black and white
Production Team:
Directed by Joseph L. Mankiewicz
Produced by Otto Lang
Screenplay by Michael Wilson, based on *Operation Cicero* by
    L.C. Moyzisch
Music by Bernard Herrmann
Cast:

| | |
|---|---|
| Diello/Cicero | James Mason |
| Countess Anna Staviska | Danielle Darrieux |
| George Travers | Michael Rennie |
| Sir Frederic | Walter Hampden |
| Ludwig Moyzisch | Oscar Karlweis |
| Colonel Von Richter | Herbert Berghof |
| Franz Von Papen | John Wengraf |

*From Russia with Love*

Distributed by United Artists, 1963
Running time 115 minutes in colour
Production Team:
Directed by Terence Young
Produced by Harry Saltzman/Albert R. Broccoli.
Screenplay by Richard Maibaum, based on the novel *From Russia with
    Love* by Ian Fleming
Music by John Barry

Cast:

| | |
|---|---|
| James Bond | Sean Connery |
| Tatianna Romanova | Daniela Bianchi |
| Rosa Klebb | Lotte Lenya |
| Ali Kerim Bey | Pedro Armendariz |
| Donald 'Red' Grant | Robert Shaw |
| 'M' | Bernard Lee |
| Miss Moneypenny | Lois Maxwell |
| Major Boothroyd | Desmond Llewelyn |

*The Guns of Navarone*

Distributed by Columbia Pictures, 1961
Running time 158 minutes in colour
Production Team:
Directed by J. Lee Thompson
Produced by Carl Foreman
Screenplay by Carl Foreman, based on the novel *The Guns of Navarone* by Alistair MacLean
Music by Dimitri Tiomkin
Cast:

| | |
|---|---|
| Keith Mallory | Gregory Peck |
| Colonel Andrea Stavrou | Anthony Quinn |
| Major Roy Franklin | Anthony Quayle |
| Corporal Miller | David Niven |
| Butcher Brown | Stanley Baker |
| Commodore Jensen | James Robertson Justice |
| Spyros Pappadimos | James Darren |
| Maria | Irene Papas |
| Anna | Gia Scala |

# BIBLIOGRAPHY

Ambler, Eric, *The Mask of Dimitrios* (Hodder & Stoughton, 1939)

Andrew, Christopher, *Secret Service* (Heinemann, 1985)

——, *The Defence of the Realm, The Authorised History of MI5* (Allen Lane, 2009)

Bassett Richard, *Hitler's Spy Chief* (Weidenfeld & Nicolson, 2005)

Bazna, Elyesa, *I was Cicero* (Andre Deutsch, 1962)

Brendon, Piers, *The Dark Valley: A Panorama of the 1930s* (Jonathan Cape, 2000)

Brown, Anthony Cave, *Body Guard of Lies* (Harper & Row Publishers, 1975)

——, *'C' The Secret life of Sir Stewart Menzies, Spymaster to Winston Churchill* (Macmillan, 1989)

Bullock, Alan, *Hitler: A Study in Tyranny* (Oldhams Press, 1953)

Burger, Adolf, *The Devil's Workshop* (Frontline Books, 2009)

Ciano, Count Galeazzo, *Ciano's Diary, 1937–1943* (Methuen & Co., 1952)

Cook, Andrew, *Ace of Spies* (The History Press, 2002)

Cooper, Artemis, *Cairo in the War, 1939–1945* (Hamish Hamilton, 1989)

Deakin, F.W. *The Brutal Friendship* (Weidenfeld & Nicolson, 1962)

Dimitrakis, Panagiotis, *Military Intelligence in Cyprus* (Tauris, 2010)

Elliott, Nicholas, *Never Judge a Man by his Umbrella* (Michael Russell, 1991)

Eppler, Johannes, *Operation Condor* (Macdonald and Janes, 1977)

Farago, Ladislas, *The Game of Foxes* (David McKay, 1971)

Fleming, Ian, *From Russia with Love* (Jonathan Cape, 1957)

Frankland, Nobel and Dowling, Christopher (eds), *Decisive Battles of the Twentieth Century* (Sedgwick & Jackson, 1976)

Freely, John, *The Companion Guide to Turkey* (Collins, 1979)

Garcia, Juan Pujol and West, Nigel, *Operation Garbo* (Weidenfeld & Nicolson, 1985)

Jeffery, Keith, *MI6: The History of the Secret Intelligence Service, 1909–1949* (Bloomsbury, 2010)

Johnson, Brian, *The Secret War* (BBC, 1978)

Jones, Nigel, *Countdown to Valkyrie* (Frontline Books, 2008)

Jorgensen, Christer, *Hitler's Espionage Machine* (The Lyons Press, 2004)

Judd, Alan, *The Quest for 'C'* (Harper Collins, 1999)

Kahn, David, *The Codebreakers* (Weidenfeld & Nicolson 1973)

——, *Hitler's Spies* (Hodder & Stoughton, 1978)

Knatchbull-Hugessen, Sir Hughe, *Diplomat in Peace and War* (John Murray, 1949)

Levine, Joshua, *Operation Fortitude* (Collins, 2011)

Lewin, Ronald, *Rommel as Military Commander* (B.T. Batsford, 1968)

Lewis, Peter, *Eric Ambler* (Frederick Ungar, 1990)

Lockhart, Robin Bruce, *Reilly: Ace of Spies* (Hodder & Stoughton, 1967)

Lucas, James, *Kommando: German Special Forces of World War Two* (Arms and Armour Press, 1985)

———, *Last Days of the Reich* (Arms and Armour Press, 1986)

Lycett, Andrew, *Ian Fleming* (Weidenfeld & Nicolson, 1995)

Macdonogh, Giles, *1938: Hitler's Gamble* (Constable, 2009)

Macintyre, Ben, *For Your Eyes Only: Ian Fleming and James Bond* (Bloomsbury, 2008)

———, *Agent Zigzag* (Bloomsbury, 2007)

———, *Double Cross: The True Story of the D-Day Spies* (Bloomsbury, 2012)

MacLean, Alistair, *The Guns of Navarone* (Collins, 1957)

Maclean, Fitzroy, *Take Nine Spies* (Atheneum, 1978)

Mason, James, *Before I Forget* (Hamish Hamilton, 1981)

Masterman, J.C., *The Double Cross System* (Yale University Press, 1972)

Mazower, Mark, *Salonica: City of Ghosts* (Harper Collins, 2004)

McKay, Sinclair, *The Secret Life of Bletchley Park* (Aurum Press, 2010)

Montagu, Ewen, *Beyond Top Secret Ultra* (Coward, McCann & Geoghegan, 1978)

Morgan, Mike, *Sting of the Scorpion* (Sutton, 2000)

Moyzisch, L.C., *Operation Cicero* (Readers Union, 1952)

Newby, Eric, *On the Shores of the Mediterranean* (Harvill Press, 1984)

———, *A Merry Dance Around the World* (Harper Collins, 1995)

Papen, Franz Von, *Memoirs* (Andre Deutsch, 1952)

Pettifer, James, *The Turkish Labyrinth: Ataturk and the New Islam* (Viking, 1997)

Philby, Kim, *My Silent War* (Macgibbon & Kee, 1968)

Pitt, Barrie, *Special Boat Squadron* (Century Publishing, 1983)

Playfair, Major General I.S.O., *The Mediterranean and Middle East, Volume II* (The Naval & Military Press, 2004)

Rankin, Nicholas. *Ian Flemings Commandos* (Faber and Faber, 2011)

Rodenbeck, Max, *Cairo, the City Victorious* (Picador, 1998)

Rogers, Anthony, *Churchill's Folly: Leros and the Aegean* (Cassell, 2003)

Sansom, A.W., *I Spied Spies* (George G.Harrap, 1965)

Schellenberg, Walter, *The Memoirs of Hitler's spymaster* (Andre Deutsch, 2006)

Sebag-Montefiore, Hugh, *Enigma: The Battle for the Code* (Weidenfeld & Nicolson, 2000)

———, *Invasion 1940* (St. Ermin's Press, 2000)

Simmons, Mark, *The Battle of Matapan 1941* (Spellmount, 2011)

———, *The Rebecca Code* (Spellmount, 2012)

Smith, Michael, *Station X* (Channel 4 Books, 1998)

Stafford, David, *Secret Agent* (BBC Books 2000)

Tsouras, Peter, *Disaster at D-Day* (Greenhill Books, 1994)

Tucker-Jones, Anthony, *Falaise: The Flawed Victory* (Pen & Sword, 2008)

Weale, Adrian, *The SS: A new history* (Little Brown, 2010)

———, *Renegades: Hitler's Englishmen* (Weidenfeld & Nicolson, 1994)

Webster Jack, *Alistair MacLean* (Chapmans, 1991)

Whiting, Charles, *Hitler's Secret War* (Leo Cooper, 2000)

Wires, Richard, *The Cicero Spy Affair* (Praeger, 1999)

Wright, Peter, *Spy Catcher* (Viking, 1987)

Young, Desmond, *Rommel: The Desert Fox* (Collins, 1950)

**Archives**
Central Intelligence Agency Centre for the Study of Intelligence
Foreign Service of the USA
Imperial War Museum
Library of Congress
Opel Museum, Berlin
Public Records Office, Kew
United States National Archives
United States Navy Historical Centre

**DVDs**
*The Guns of Navarone* (Columbia Pictures)
*Five Fingers* (Twentieth Century Fox)
*From Russia with Love* (United Artists)

**Journals and Newspapers**
*Daily Mail*
*Daily Telegraph*
*Medal News Magazine*
*New York Times*
*Sunday Express*
*Sunday Times*
*The Times*
*World War II Magazine*
*World War II Quarterly*

# NOTES

The following abbreviations have been used:

| | |
|---|---|
| Central Intelligence Agency Library/OSS | CIAL |
| Foreign Office (British) | FO |
| Foreign Service (USA) | FS |
| National Archives (USA) | NA |
| Security service Files | KV |
| Public Records Office | PRO |
| War Office | WO |

## Prologue

1  KV 6/8 United States First Army report, 13/5/1945
2  KV 6/8 Interrogation M. Molkenteller, p.3
3  *Ibid.*, p.6
4  KV 6/8 Statement M. Molkenteller, p.3
5  *Ibid.*, p.4
6  KV 6/8 Security Service letter, 25/5/1945
7  KV 6/8 Security Service letter, 12/7/1945

## 1 First Contact, 1943

1  Moyzisch, L.C., *Operation Cicero*, p.29
2  *Ibid.*, p.30
3  Bazna, E., *I was Cicero*, p.46
4  Moyzisch, p.30
5  KV 6/8 Moyzisch interrogation 19A
6  Von Papen, Franz, *Memoirs*, pp.509–10
7  Bazna, p.52
8  Moyzisch, p.31
9  Bazna, p.14
10 Moyzisch, pp.31–4
11 *Ibid.*, p.35.
12 Wires, Richard, *The Cicero Spy Affair*, p.6
13 Moyzisch, p.35.
14 Pettifer, James, *The Turkish Labyrinth Ataturk and the New Islam*, p.57
15 *Ibid.*, p.68
16 Moyzisch, p.36
17 Schellenberg, Walter, *The Memoirs of Hitler's Spymaster*, pp.380–1
18 *Ibid.*, p.382

## 2 Elyesa Bazna

1  Ambler, Eric, *The Mask of Dimitrios*, p.1
2  Mazower, Mark, *Salonica*, p.296
3  Bazna, p.12

4 *Ibid.*, p.13
5 Pettifer, p.5
6 Bazna, p.15
7 *Ibid.*, p.16.
8 *Ibid.*, pp.16–7
9 *Ibid.*, pp.19–20
10 *Ibid.*, pp.24–5

11 Wires, p.33
12 Bazna, p.36
13 KV 6/8 Cicero Summary
14 Bazna, pp.44–5
15 Von Papen, p.510
16 Bazna, p.46

## 3 Berlin Decides

1 Moyzisch, p.36
2 *Ibid.*, p.37
3 Bazna, p.48
4 Von Papen, p.67
5 *Ibid.*, p.162
6 *Ibid.*, p.162
7 Bullock, Alan, *Hitler: A Study in Tyranny*, p.232. Also see p.323: 'Only three of the eleven posts were held by the Nazis and apart from the chancellorship both were second-rate positions'
8 Von Papen, p.317
9 Bullock, p.281. Also see Von Papen, p.281
10 Von Papen, p.437
11 *Ibid.*, p.438
12 *Ibid.*, p.439
13 *Ibid.*, p.440

14 *Ibid.*, p.444
15 Ciano, Count Galeazzo, *Diary: 1937–1943*, p.233. Also see Deakin, F.W., *The Brutal Friendship*, p.174
16 Von Papen, p.445
17 *Ibid.*, p.446
18 KV 6/8 C507784
19 Knatchbull-Hugessen, Sir Hughe, *Diplomat in Peace and War*, pp.150–1
20 Von Papen, p.486
21 *Ibid.*, p.486
22 *Ibid.*, p.487
23 Moyzisch, pp.38–9
24 *Ibid.*, p.40
25 Schellenberg, Walter, *Invasion 1940*, pp.122–3
26 Moyzisch, p.41
27 *Ibid.*, p.44
28 *Ibid.*, p.45

## 4 Second Meeting

1 Bazna, p.54
2 *Ibid.*, pp.38–41
3 *Ibid.*, p.41
4 *Ibid.*, p.57
5 Moyzisch, pp.131–2
6 Bazna, p.58
7 Von Papen, pp.509–10

8 Moyzisch, p.45
9 Bazna, pp.59–60
10 Moyzisch, p.47
11 *Ibid.*, pp.49–51
12 Bazna, pp.62–3
13 Moyzisch, p.53
14 *Ibid.*, p.55

## 5 They Called Him Cicero

1 Moyzisch, pp.58–9
2 Von Papen, p.510
3 Wires, p.44. Also see: 'had [Moyzisch] just invented the story to make his account a little more dramatic'
4 KV 6/8 C507784 note
5 Von Papen, p.511
6 Moyzisch, p.61
7 *Ibid.*, p.63

8 Bazna, p.64
9 MacLean, Fitzroy, *Take Nine Spies*, p.198
10 Bazna, pp.63–4
11 Moyzisch, pp.68–9
12 *Ibid.*, p.70
13 *Ibid.*, p.72

## 6 Who is Cicero?

1 Moyzisch, p.74
2 *Ibid.*, p.77
3 *Ibid.*, p.78
4 Von Papen, pp.493–4
5 Dimitrakis, Panagiotis, *Military Intelligence in Cyprus*, p.49
6 WO Report HS 3/118 TNA Special Operations Executive files
7 Moyzisch, pp.80–2
8 Weale, Adrian, *The SS: A New History*, p.141
9 KV 2/95 SD
10 Weale, p.142
11 Moyzisch, pp.84–5
12 *Ibid.*, p.85
13 *Ibid.*, p.90
14 *Ibid.*, pp.91–2
15 Wires, p.65
16 Moyzisch, pp.92–4
17 Ibid., pp.94–6.
18 Von Papen, p.500
19 Moyzisch, pp.96–100
20 Schellenberg, p.391
21 *Ibid.*, p.392
22 Playfair, Major General I.S.O., *The Mediterranean and Middle East, Vol II*
23 Simmons, Mark, *The Rebecca Code*, pp.60–1
24 Eppler, Johannes, *Operation Condor*, p.168
25 Moyzisch, pp.102–3
26 Wires, p.80
27 Von Papen, p.508
28 Moyzisch, pp.105–6
29 Von Papen, p.508

## 7 Around Ankara

1 Pettifer, p.51
2 Moyzisch, p.108
3 *Ibid.*, p.108
4 Von Papen, p.511
5 Moyzisch, p.108
6 *Ibid.*, pp.109–11
7 Bazna, p.71
8 *Ibid.*, p.72
9 Schellenberg, p.393
10 Wires, p.122
11 Kahn, David, p.230
12 Moyzisch, pp.114–5
13 Bazna, p.67
14 *Ibid.*, p.81
15 *Ibid.*, p.76
16 Moyzisch, p.115
17 *Ibid.*, pp.116–7

## 8 Andreas to Bernhard

1 Moyzisch, pp.117–8
2 Simmons, *The Rebecca Code*, p.138
3 Sansom, A.W., *I Spied Spies*, p.113
4 Macintyre, Ben, *Agent Zigzag*, pp.101–2
5 PRO KYZ/104, p.16
6 FS NARA, note 29/2/1940
7 Burger, Adolf, *The Devil's Workshop*, p.139
8 Schellenberg, p.222
9 Basset, Richard, *Hitler's Spy Chief*, pp.235–6
10 *Ibid.*, p.237
11 Weale, p.150
12 Burger, p.139
13 *Ibid.*, p.143
14 *Ibid.*, p.143
15 Pirie, Anthony, *Operation Bernhard*, p.119
16 Schellenberg, p.419
17 Schellenberg, Walter, *The Labyrinth*, p.368
18 Wires, p.88
19 Burger, p.160
20 *Ibid.*, p.221
21 *Ibid.*, p.225
22 *Ibid.*, p.281
23 Wires, p.92
24 Burger, p.149

## 9 December 1943

1 Moyzisch, p.120
2 Bazna, p.75
3 *The Times* 9/8/1938
4 Pettifer, p.60
5 Knatchbull-Hugessen, p.183
6 *Ibid.*, p.194
7 Bazna, p.81
8 *Ibid.*, p.82
9 *Sunday Express* 15/1/1950
10 Bazna, p.86
11 KV 6/8, p.4

12 *Ibid.*, p.5
13 Von Papen, p.511
14 Moyzisch, pp.120–1
15 *Ibid.*, p.123
16 *Ibid.*, pp.125–6
17 Bazna, pp.79–80
18 Moyzisch, p.130
19 Brown, Antony Cave, *Bodyguard of Lies*, p.435

## 10 Churchill's Folly

1 Knatchbull-Hugessen, p.186
2 *Ibid.*, p.187
3 *Ibid.*, p.190
4 KV 6/8, pp.3–4.
5 Von Papen, p.495
6 WO 32/11430
7 Rogers, Anthony, *Churchill's Folly*, p.29

8 *Ibid.*, p.83
9 PRO Air 41/53
10 FO 954/32
11 Rogers, p.80
12 Knatchbull-Hugessen, p.193
13 Brown, pp.436–7

## 11 The Turkish Labyrinth

1 Knatchbull-Hugessen, p.196
2 *Ibid.*, p.197
3 *Ibid.*, p.198
4 Cooper, Artemis, *Cairo in the War, 1939–1945*, pp.281–2
5 Sansom, p.165
6 Cooper, p.283. Also see FO 921/134
7 Knatchbull-Hugessen, p.198
8 PRO Air 20/4971. Also see Wires, p.112
9 Wires, p.112

10 Knatchbull-Hugessen, p.199
11 *Ibid.*, p.200
12 Von Papen, pp.517–8
13 Knatchbull-Hugessen, p.200
14 Von Papen, pp.511–2
15 KV 6/8, p.4. Also see Moyzisch, p.138
16 Moyzisch, pp.138–9
17 *Ibid.*, p.139
18 Von Papen, p.515
19 Moyzisch, pp.139–40

## 12 A Transfer of Affections

1 Bazna, p.67
2 *Ibid.*, p.83
3 *Ibid.*, p.89.
4 *Ibid.*, p.90
5 KV 6/8. Also see Bazna, p.1
6 Bazna, pp.93–4
7 KV 6/8, p.5
8 Bazna, p.108
9 *Ibid.*, p.109
10 *Ibid.*, p.116

11 Moyzisch, p.133
12 *Ibid.*, pp.135–6
13 Schellenberg, p.392
14 Schaffer, Ronald, *Wings of Judgment*
15 Wires, p.121
16 Moyzisch, p.150
17 Von Papen, p.511
18 Schellenberg, p.396
19 Moyzisch, p.140

## 13 To Catch a Spy

1 KV 6/8 (8)
2 Brown, pp.445–6
3 CIAL OSS documents 1466–1505
  29/12/43–1/1/44
4 Brown, p.447.
5 Andrew, Christopher, *Secret Service*,
  pp.357–8
6 Wires, p.239
7 Philby, Kim, *My Silent War*, pp.63–5
8 Simmons, Mark, *The Battle of
  Matapan, 1941*, p.30. Also see West,
  Nigel, *GCHQ: The Secret Wireless War,
  1900–1986*
9 KV 6/8 (13)
10 Andrew, p.484
11 *Ibid.*, p.408
12 Maclean, p.212
13 Wires, p.131

14 KV 6/8 (5–6)
15 *Ibid.* (6, note 15)
16 Bazna, pp.96–7
17 KV 6/8 (16)
18 Knatchbull-Hugessen, p.64
19 Farago, Ladislas, *The Game of the Foxes*,
  p.415. When Knatchbull-Hugessen.
  Also see *B.Diensl* cipher bureau Naval
  High Command and SD files
20 KV 6/8 (16)
21 MacLean, p.220. Also see Wires, p.132
22 Bazna, pp.110–2
23 Moyzisch, p.151
24 *Ibid.*, p.154
25 Bazna, pp.112–4
26 *Ibid.*, p.114
27 KV 6/8

## 14 Defections

1 Moyzisch, p.23
2 *Ibid.*, p.24
3 Von Papen, p.512
4 Moyzisch, pp.140–1. Also see Wires,
  p.168
5 *Ibid.*, pp.141–2
6 *Ibid.*, p.142. Also see Bazna, p.140 and
  Wires, p.168
7 Bazna, p.137
8 Moyzisch, p.144
9 Pettifer, p.54
10 Von Papen, p.520
11 Moyzisch, p.155
12 Von Papen, p.520. Also see Moyzisch,
  p.155

13 Bassett, p.279
14 Von Papen, p.520
15 Brown, p.435
16 Newby, Eric, *On the Shores of the
  Mediterranean*, p.192
17 Jeffery, Keith, *MI6*, p.504–5
18 Bassett, p.281–82
19 *Ibid.*, p.282
20 Schellenberg, p.399
21 Von Papen, p.520–21
22 Moyzisch, p 155–56
23 *Ibid.*, p.157
24 Bazna, p.136–37

## 15 Cicero's Later Period

1 Moyzisch, p.149
2 Bazna, p.141
3 *Ibid.*, p.120
4 USNA German Foreign Ministry
  records 10/2/1944. Also see Wires,
  p.155. The valet later claimed that
  Jenke had told him that Hitler
  planned to reward him with a villa
5 Moyzisch, pp.166–7
6 KV 6/8, p.7

7 *Ibid.*, L305/Gov/72
8 Moyzisch, p.203
9 Von Papen, p.521
10 *Ibid.*, p.521
11 KV 6/8, p.15
12 Wires, p.161
13 Moyzisch, p.166
14 Bazna, p.134
15 KV 6/8 (45), p.12
16 Moyzisch, p.165. Also see Bazna, p.135

17 Jeffery, p.504. Also see Elliot, *Never Judge*, p.134
18 KV 6/8 (45), p.12

## 16 Another Spy
1 Moyzisch, p.142
2 Farago, p.489
3 Bazna, p.100. Also see Wires, p.166
4 *Ibid.*, pp.100–1
5 Moyzisch, p.140
6 Bazna, p.100
7 *Ibid.*, p.104
8 CIAL Intelligence, VI, 4–48
9 *Ibid.*, VI, 49
10 *Ibid.*, VI, 49
11 Moyzisch, p.157
12 Bazna, p.101
13 *Ibid.*, p.102
14 *Ibid.*, p.99
15 KV 6/8 Interrogation Summing up 30/5/1944, p.17

19 Cave, pp.448–9
20 Moyzisch, p.166

16 Bazna, p.142
17 Moyzisch, pp.169–70. Also Bazna, pp.141–2
18 Bazna, pp.140–1
19 Moyzisch, p.161
20 *Ibid.*, pp.168–9
21 *Ibid.*, p.176
22 *Ibid.*, pp.26–8
23 *Ibid.*, p.172. Also see KV 6/8
24 KV 6/8
25 Moyzisch, pp.172–3
26 *Ibid.*, p.177. Also see Bazna, p.159
27 Bazna, p.138
28 Moyzisch, pp.143–64
29 *Ibid.*, p.178

## 17 Two Spies Bow Out
1 Bazna, pp.145 and 153–4
2 Brown, p.446
3 Bazna, pp.146–7
4 Moyzisch, pp.179–80
5 Bazna, p.160
6 Moyzisch, pp.180–1
7 Bazna, p.160
8 Moyzisch, pp.183–4
9 *Ibid.*, p.186

10 Bazna, p.149
11 *Ibid.*, pp.152–5
12 CIAL Intelligence, VI, pp.4–51
13 *Ibid.*, VI, p.52
14 Moyzisch, p.192
15 *Ibid.*, p.192. Also see Bazna, pp.156–7
16 Bazna, pp.165–8

## 18 The Fallout
1 Bazna, p.160
2 KV 6/8, p.5
3 CIAL Intelligence, VI, 4–52
4 Bazna, p.160
5 KV 6/8 Interrogation summary
6 *Ibid.*
7 CIAL Intelligence, VI, 4–52
8 Moyzisch, pp.186–7
9 *Ibid.*, pp.188–90
10 *Ibid.*, pp.191–2

11 *Ibid.*, p.197
12 Von Papen, p.524
13 *Ibid.*, pp.524–5
14 Knatchbull-Hugessen, p.202. Also see Wires, p.181
15 *Ibid.*, p.202
16 KV 6/8 Minute sheet 10
17 Bazna, p.171
18 *Ibid.*, pp.168–9

## 19 The Longest Day
1 Bazna, pp.73–5. Also see Moyzisch, p.164
2 Bullock, p.679. Also see Farago, p.597

3 Rankin, Nicholas, *Ian Fleming's Commandos*, p.19

4 Frankland, Noble and Dowling, Christopher (eds), *Decisive Battles of the Twentieth Century*, p.270
5 *Ibid.*, p.271
6 KV 6/8 (45) and p.12
7 Brown, XI
8 *Ibid.*, p.446
9 *Ibid.*, p.447
10 *Ibid.*, p.448
11 *Ibid.*, p.449
12 MacLean, p.221
13 KV 6/8. Also see FO File 850
14 Wires, p.136
15 Andrew, p.488
16 Philby, p.47
17 Levine, Joshua, *Operation Fortitude*, p.12
18 Simmons, *Matapan*, p.154
19 Andrew, pp.487–8
20 Macintyre, Ben, *Double Cross*, p.35
21 Levine, p.67

23 Farago, p.597
24 Lewin, Ronald, *Rommel as Military Commander*, p.213. Also see Young, Desmond, *Rommel: The Desert Fox*, pp.211–2
24 Frankland and Dowling, p.271
25 Von Papen, p.525
26 Bullock, p.679
27 Brown, Anthony Cave, 'C', p.560
28 Macintyre, p.249. Also see Masterman, J.C., *The Double-Cross System*, p.156
29 *Ibid.*, pp.74–5
30 Farago, p.624
31 Lewin, p.223
32 Farago, pp.624–5. Also see three German signals Abw/4508/43, RSHA IV-A2/478/44 and RSHA IV-a2/573/44
33 Andrew, p.488
34 Kahn, David, *Hitler's Spies*, p.328
35 KV 6/8, p.15

## 20 War's End

1 Von Papen, p.527
2 Wires, p.180
3 Jones, Nigel, *Countdown to Valkyrie*, pp.192–3
4 Von Papen, pp.529–30
5 Moyzisch, p.200
6 Bazna, pp.176–7
7 *Ibid.*, p.180

8 Von Papen, pp.530–2
9 Knatchbull-Hugessen, p.217
10 *Ibid.*, p.223
11 Moyzisch, pp.200–1
12 KV 6/8 Moyzisch Interrogation, p.4
13 Von Papen, p.533
14 *Ibid.*, p.535
15 *Ibid.*, p.536

## 21 Trial and Revelation

1 Wires, p.185. Also see Bazna, p.186
2 Bazna, p.187
3 KV 6/8 1/7/1945
4 *Ibid.*, 19/6/1945
5 Schellenberg, pp.393–4
6 Moyzisch, p.201
7 Von Papen, pp.537–8
8 *Ibid.*, pp.547–8
9 *Ibid.*, p.551
10 *Ibid.*, p.578
11 Schellenberg, pp.14–5
12 Knatchbull-Hugessen, p.ix
13 KV 6/8 Copy *Sunday Express*
14 *Ibid.*, John Prebble Copy *Sunday Express*

15 Wires, p.182
16 KV 6/8 Minute Sheet Y Box 6351. Also see CIAL Intelligence, VI, pp.4–47
17 Moyzisch, p.207
18 *Five Fingers*, Twentieth Century-Fox, 1952
19 Bazna, p.188
20 *Ibid.*, p.189
21 *Ibid.*, p.189
22 *Ibid.*, p.5
23 *Ibid.*, pp.5–6
24 *Ibid.*, p.183
25 KV 6/8 Report 11/62
26 CIAL Intelligence, VI, pp.4–52. Also see Bazna, pp.183–4

27 Bazna, pp.106 and 183–4. See Also
  Kahn, p.591
28 Wires, p.177
29 *Ibid.*, p.187

30 KV 6/8 Summary of Cicero
  Case 1979 for History of British
  Intelligence in WW2, p.8

## 22  Stellar Spy

1 Kahn, p.354
2 MacLean, p.221. Also see Wires, p.192
3 KV 6/8 p.6
4 *Ibid.*
5 Simmons, *Matapan*, p.85
6 McKay, Sinclair, *The Secret Life of
  Bletchley Park*, p.174
7 Moyzisch, p.110
8 Wires, p.195
9 Bazna, p.167
10 Moyzisch, p.203

11 KV 6/8 Statement M.
  Molkenteller, p.3
12 KV 6/8 p.4
13 Wires, p.199
14 Wright, Peter, *Spy Catcher*, p.78
15 CIAL Footnote to Cicero 'One of her
  first contacts …', p.48
16 Wires, p.202
17 Moyzisch, pp.202–3
18 *Ibid.*, p.204
19 Von Papen, pp.517–8

## 23  Cicero in Fiction

1 Ambler, p.116
2 CIAL intelligence, VI, 4–47
3 Simmons, *The Rebecca Code*, pp.7–8
4 *Five Fingers*, Twentieth Century Fox,
  1952
5 Wires, p.188
6 Mason, James, *Before I forget*, p.224
7 *Five Fingers*, Twentieth Century Fox,
  1952
8 *The Times* 10/03/1952
9 Mason, p.224
10 Moyzisch, p.24
11 Von Papen, p.512
12 Wires, p.177
13 Bazna, p.138
14 *Ibid.*, pp.140 and 143–4.
15 *Ibid.*, pp.171–3

16 Macintyre, Ben, *For Your Eyes Only*,
  p.93
17 Fleming, Ian, *From Russia with Love*,
  p.109
18 *Ibid.*, p.192
19 Lycett, Andrew, *Ian Fleming*, pp.382–3
20 *The Guns of Navarone*, Columbia
  Pictures, 1961
21 Webster, Jack, *Alistair MacLean*, p.40
22 *Ibid.*, pp.92–3
23 Mason, p.224. Also see Wires, p.191.
  *Five Fingers* so cleverly mixed actual
  events with rumours and fanciful
  notions

# INDEX

Visit our website and discover thousands of other History Press books.

**www.thehistorypress.co.uk**